Simple Truth Daily Devotions

Daily Reminders for Living God's Word

A Yearly Devotional

Susan Ray

Front Cover Photo by Anna Ray

Simple Truth Daily Devotions

FOREWORD

I grew up believing in God! I remember learning about Him at a very early age. I remember many things I was taught in church, in Sunday School and by my parents. Growing up, however, I did not attend church very much. I tried to do what was right, but did not always follow God's ways. It wasn't until I was much older, that I realized in order to do the right things, I needed to follow God's ways all of the time. I learned that I needed to not only believe in God, but I needed to have a relationship with Jesus. I'm not perfect and I don't always do what's right every time, but with Jesus in my life, I have found the hope that I need to keep trying. The wonderful thing about knowing Jesus, is that it's hard keeping this wonderful news to myself. That is exactly why I wrote this book! At first, I wanted to share what I knew with my children. Before long, I wanted to share His truths with everyone. I pray you are renewed by these reminders and that they help you begin spending valuable time in His word daily.

God Bless You,

Susan

"...you exude what God wants us to do here on this earth! I can't even begin to tell you the blessing that you have been in starting your devotional." Kim Decher Smith

"Thank you for the words of encouragement and Godly direction." Melinda Wardle

"Susan, your writing is so beautiful! Thank you for sharing!" Sue Ann Yovanovich

DEDICATION

To Jimmy and Anna Ray. You were the inspiration I needed to begin writing these devotions. You were and still are my reason for wanting to be a better person. I pray daily that you will continue your walk, with Jesus by your side. I pray you never forget these simple, but very important truths.

I love you with all my heart!!
Mom

James 1:18 (NCV) "God decided to give us life through the word of truth so we might be the most important of all things he made."

4

January 1

A New Year, A Fresh Start

Like newly fallen snow, you have the chance to make new footprints in your life. May you see each new day as a chance to make wise choices. Look to your creator for all your decisions. Start each day, with fresh thoughts in His word and make each footprint count.

Psalm 20:4 "May He give you the desire of your heart and make all your plans succeed."

Proverbs 16:3 "Commit to the Lord whatever you do, and your plans will succeed."

January 2

Cry Out to the Lord

There will be moments in your life, when you will go through tough times. Remember though, it is through those times that you will grow stronger. Drawing closer to God, through prayer, will allow your relationship with Him to grow. When you need God the most, may you find comfort in those daily conversations with Him. Cry out to the Lord!

Psalm 34:17 "The righteous cry out, and the Lord hears them; He delivers them from all their troubles."

James 4:8 "Come near to God and He will come near to you."

January 3

Where Does the Time Go?

You will have lazy days, crazy days and days when you don't know how you will ever get it all done. Remember, though, that no matter what kind of day you are having, you will always have someone on your side who will help you. When you need help turn to Him for direction. Through it all, God hears your prayers.

Psalm 4:1 "Answer me when I call to you, O, my righteous God. Give me relief from my distress; be merciful to me and hear my prayers."

January 4

The Glass Is Half Full

When you are struggling, or having a bad day, remember the glass could be half empty or half full. It is up to you to decide how you see things. Look for the positive in all situations and trust in Him. Let God know you need Him to guide you in a better direction. Call on Him to help you see the glass as half full.

Psalm 18:3 "I call to the Lord, who is worthy of praise, and I am saved from my enemies."

Philippians 2:5 "Your attitude should be the same as that of Jesus Christ."

January 5

Our Time on This Earth

Our days will go by, like the blink of an eye. What we need to do each day is prepare for our time in Heaven. Don't get caught up with things of this world that will fade away. Hold on to His promises! Spend your time doing something worthwhile. Focus on what's important! When you spend your time focusing on God, it will help you look at your life differently.

2 Corinthians 4:18 "So we fix our eyes not on what is seen, but on what is unseen. For what is seen is temporary, but what is unseen is eternal."

January 6

Don't Give Up

When you are tired and don't think you can keep going, don't give up! Look to God and ask Him to give you the strength to do all things. Remember each day that He is near you and will never leave you. With God on your side, imagine how much more you'll feel like doing. When you make God first in your life, you'll be amazed at what you are able to do.

Philippians 4:13 "I can do everything through Him who gives me strength."

January 7

The Loss of a Loved One

When you've lost a loved one, you may find yourself wondering how you can go on. God placed us on this earth for a reason and each of us has our own purpose. Pray God will help you remain on the right path to your purpose. May it comfort you to know, that your loved one will be waiting for you when you leave this earth. Until then, they will be cheering for you to complete the purpose they were once a part of.

1 Corinthians 12:6 "There are different kinds of working, but the same God works all of them in all men."

Romans 8:28 "And we know that in all things God works for the good of those who love Him, who have been called according to His purpose."

January 8

Forgive One Another

No one is perfect and unfortunately; we all make mistakes. With that in mind, there will be times when you want to be forgiven for something you have said or done. You must also forgive others when you think or feel that you have been done wrong. Live your life treating others the way you would like to be treated. Forgive one another!

Colossians 2:13 "When you were dead in your sins and…your sinful nature, God made you alive with Christ. He forgave us all our sins."

Colossians 3:13 "Bear with each other and forgive whatever grievances you may have against one another. Forgive as the Lord forgave you."

January 9

Work Hard Every Day

Work hard every day! Give it your all, as if you are working for Jesus. Whatever you are doing, do it joyfully, as if you are a servant in Heaven. When you work with a servant's heart, good news will travel because of your joyfulness. Others will want to know how you are able to do so much. They will want to know where your JOY comes from.

Colossians 3:23 "Whatever you do, work at it with all your heart, as working for the Lord, not for human masters."

John 12:26 "Whoever serves me must follow me; and where I am, my servant also will be. My Father will honor the one who serves me."

Jesus
Others
You

January 10

Volunteer Your Time

There is no question that your time is important. In this busy world, we are often pulled in many directions. There is no better feeling though, than helping others. You could do a little extra at work or really get involved by volunteering your time to a worthy cause. The feeling you will get, from a job well done and a little extra time spent helping others, will go a long way.

1 Samuel 12:24 "But be sure to fear the Lord and serve Him faithfully with all your heart; consider what great things He has done for you."

Luke 18:27 "What is impossible with men is possible with God."

January 11

Live with a Giving Heart

Isn't it wonderful knowing that God will provide for you? Sometimes, it is hard to know what will happen, if you tithe or donate money, when you are not sure of your next pay check. What if you are living paycheck to paycheck? Live with a giving heart and you will be amazed at how God can show you what you truly need. He comes through at just the right time. Live with a giving heart and watch God at work.

Matthew 6:11 "Give us this day our daily bread."

Proverbs 3:9-10 "Honor the Lord with your wealth, with the firstfruits of all your crops; then your barns will be filled to overflowing..."

January 12

Be Truthful to Yourself

We are all sinners! We need to admit that we are sinners and we should ask for God's help. Pray to God! Tell Him you want to be a better person. Tell Him you want to learn to be more Christlike. When we confess our sins, we grow to be more aware of them. We can learn to be in control of ourselves and our habits, by asking for help.

Proverbs 28:13 "He who conceals his sins does not prosper, but whoever confesses and renounces them finds mercy."

January 13

Don't Be Too Hard on Yourself

Don't be too hard on yourself, God isn't! He loves you no matter what. God will never stop loving you. He made you to be the type of person He wants you to be. You have the ability to do and be so much. Isn't it wonderful that you can have someone on your side, that just wants you to be yourself? He loves you, even when you aren't so sure of yourself? Ask God to help you be the best that you can be.

Ephesians 5:1-2 "Be imitators of God, therefore, as dearly loved children and live a life of love, just as Christ loved us and gave himself up for us as a fragrant offering and sacrifice to God."

January 14

You Are Never Alone

There are times when we feel like we are all alone. We are trying to do everything by ourselves and making decisions on our own. The good news is, we are never alone. Even when "man" lets us down, God is by our side. He will listen to our needs and put us in the right direction. When you feel alone, ask God to help you feel His presence. Ask Him to point you in the right direction. Ask Him to help you know, that you are never alone.

Hebrews 13:5 "…Never will I leave you; never will I forsake you."

January 15

Don't Judge One Another

No one is perfect, not me, not you...so how can we look at another person and question what they do or don't do? We each have things in our lives we could probably do better. We have thoughts we could change and attitudes we could improve. The next time we think about judging someone, let's pray that it's for a contest or a performance. Let us not judge anyone for who they are or who they are not.

Matthew 7:1 "Do not judge, or you too will be judged."

January 16

Don't Worry

Worrying takes up so much time and energy, so why do we do it? We worry because we do not know what lies ahead for us. We worry because we might be lacking in our faith. Test yourself with this...keep track of how many times your worries don't turn out the way you thought they would anyway. How often are you worried for no reason? You'll be amazed at how many times God takes care of those worries and turns them into something remarkable. Something that you wouldn't have imagined, but are so thankful for.

Matthew 6:34 "Therefore do not worry about tomorrow, for tomorrow will worry about itself."

January 17

Do Not Be Afraid

Do not fear challenges that lie ahead for you. God has a plan for you and He wants you to succeed. If we look to Him for His guidance, He will give us the confidence we need, so we will not be fearful of anything or anyone. With your trust in Him, you'll be able to set aside your fears and persevere.

Proverbs 29:25 "Fear of man will prove to be a snare, but whoever trusts in the Lord is kept safe."

2 Timothy 1:7 "For God did not give us a spirit of timidity, but a spirit of power, of love and of self-discipline."

January 18 (Part 1)

He Wants You to Turn to Him

Admitting you cannot do it on your own, is not a sign of weakness, it is a sign of faith. God wants us to come to Him in our time of need. He cares for us and loves us so much. He loves when His children call on Him. Turn your worries over to Him, turn it all over to Him.

1 Peter 5:7 "Cast all your anxiety on Him because He cares for you."

January 19 (Part 2)

When I am Weak

2 Corinthians 12:10 ends by saying "For when I am weak, then I am strong."

I love being reminded of this, because it is so true. We shine at our weakest moments. When we admit our weaknesses, we are showing others that we are real. Forgiving or apologizing to someone when you are wrong shows them the true you, so others can see you in a brighter light. When God is in your heart and you are not afraid to show your weaknesses, think of how others will see that reflection of confidence and self-control. They will want to know more about the power you have within you.

2 Corinthians 12:9 "My grace is made perfect in weakness."

January 20

He Will Lift You Up

There may be days you feel left out or feel you should have been noticed for something good you did. God knows what you did. He also knows your heart and how you feel. We will not fully be satisfied with "man's" award anyway. Our rewards will come from God alone and His grace. Be patient, "He will lift you up!"

James 4:10 "Humble yourselves before the Lord and He will lift you up."

January 21

Keep the Faith

Faith is...believing in what you can't see because of what you can see. We cannot see God, but when we believe, we can see what God is capable of. A small miracle like missing the accident by a few seconds because of the few extra minutes you spent at that light. A greater miracle, like when your prayers are answered and your friend is healed. There are no coincidences but there is Faith when you trust in Him.

Finding strength in
All things by
Increasing my
Trust in
Him

Hebrews 11:1 "Now faith is confidence in what we hope for and assurance about what we do not see."

John 20:29 "...blessed are those who have not seen and yet have believed."

January 22

Obey Your Mother and Father

We are brought up from babies by our mothers and fathers. When we are young, we do not always realize the sacrifices they are making. They love us and would do anything for us. Many times, we do not even notice they are doing it all for us, until we are much older. Sometimes it is too late when we realize how much they truly did for us. Treasure each moment and respect and obey them, as God would want you to do.

Deuteronomy 5:16 "Honor your father and your mother, as the Lord, your God has commanded you, so that you may live long and that it may go well with you in the land the Lord your God is giving you."

January 23

God Has a Plan

Most of the time, you probably feel like you know how your days will go. Some days will go as planned. However, you will have other days, that won't go as you had thought. Know that God has a plan for you. He has a plan for all of us and sometimes that plan will not match what we have in mind. Don't get discouraged though, ask God to help you trust in Him. Ask Him to help you be open to His plan. It may not be what you had in mind, but you'll be thankful in the long run and glad you put your trust in Him.

Proverbs 3:6 "...in all your ways acknowledge Him, and He will make your paths straight."

January 24

You Win Some, You Lose Some

Winning is fun, but you can also have a good time playing, when you know you've done your best. Sometimes it will be in God's plan for you to win, but sometimes it's in His plan for you to lose. Win or lose, you still need to be the same person with the same attitude. Be a reflection of God, by winning or losing with a positive attitude. Be thankful for the chance you have to give it your all.

2 Samuel 22:36 "You give me your shield of victory; you stoop down to make me great."

January 25

Pray About Everything

Don't get discouraged about anything, but pray about everything. If you are unsure which direction to take, pray! When you don't know what to say, pray! God wants you to turn to Him in your time of need. He wants you to get close to Him. Praying regularly will help you get closer to Him and will help you have that relationship you are longing for, and God is waiting for.

1 Thessalonians 5:16-18 "Be joyful always; pray continually; give thanks in all circumstances, for this is God's will for you in Christ Jesus."

January 26

Do Not Gossip

Watch what you say about one another and be sure you never gossip. Sometimes you will hear things and you will be tempted to tell others. Remember, though, that God does not want you to talk about others that way. Would you want others to talk about you? Spreading good news is one thing, but saying things that aren't very nice, is never wise. Spread cheer not gossip!

Proverbs 11:13 "A gossip betrays a confidence, but a trustworthy man keeps a secret."

January 27

No Pain, No Gain

We all know the saying, "no pain, no gain," but what does it really mean? Life is going to be hard at times and we are going to struggle. It is through those times, though, that we grow. We gain confidence, we gain courage and we gain strength. When we pray to God for help through the tough times, He shows us the way, so we can come out stronger...better! He doesn't promise it will be pain-free, but with each obstacle, we gain the wisdom we need, to get through those times, each time.

Philippians 4:7 "And the peace of God, which transcends all understanding will guard your hearts and your minds in Christ Jesus."

1 Peter 5:10 "And the God of all grace, who called you to His eternal glory in Christ, after you have suffered a little while, will Himself restore you and make you strong, firm and steadfast."

January 28

Praying for Others

When you are worried about your family and friends and hoping they will get to know Christ better, pray for them. Ask God to come into their hearts. Ask Him to give you the words to speak, so that you are able to share your good news with them. Pray they will see the changes in you and the faith you have. Pray that they will want to hear what God has done for you, what He has done for all of us.

Psalms 66:16 "Come and listen, all you who fear God; let me tell you what He has done for me."

January 29

Don't Take Matters into Your Own Hands

When you are trying to figure out what to do in a situation where man has done you wrong, don't take matters into your own hands. God is waiting for you to ask Him for help. You can pray for the other person or people that wronged you, but you can also pray for peace and contentment. Remember, God has a plan for you! In time and through prayer and patience, you'll be able to see it as God wants you to see it. Until then, do not try to fix it yourself.

Proverbs 20:22 "Do not say 'I'll pay you back for this wrong!' Wait for the Lord, and He will deliver you."

January 30

Be Respectful

Above all else, respect yourself and respect others. In order to show how great God is, you should always be your best. God wants you to treat others with respect. Sometimes that means holding back from something you were going to say. It always means putting others first. When you think before you speak, you'll feel better in the long run and others will put their trust in you. More importantly, if they know they can come to you and be treated with respect, think of how wonderful it will be for them, when they trust and turn to Him because of that respect.

Luke 6:31 "Do to others as you would have them do to you."

January 31

Loving Everyone

It is easy to love someone who is lovable and good to you. What about those who are harder to love? How do you handle and treat them? God wants us to love everyone, our enemies included. I know at times, you will wonder how you can do that, but with God you can. Come to Him and ask Him to help you find it in you, to see the good in them. If there are attitudes that need changed, ask Him to help those attitudes be changed. Whether it is your attitude or theirs, it can be done. Imagine how your reward will be even greater, when you are able to love everyone.

Luke 6:35 "But love your enemies, do good to them, and lend to them without expecting to get anything back. Then your reward will be great..."

February 1

Compliment Don't Criticize

Sometimes, we are our own worst critics. We find our faults and focus on them, even when we have done well. Because of this, we need to lift each other up. Tell your friends and family the good things about them, regularly. Compliment them each chance you get. By doing this, you are not only lifting them up, you are being a reflection of God. After all, isn't being Christlike, the way you should be?

1 Thessalonians 5:11 "Therefore encourage one another and build each other up, just as in fact you are doing."

February 2

Be Positive

Each day, we should look for the good in people in all situations. When the game doesn't go the way you would have liked, don't focus on the loss, focus on the positive. Did you have fun? Was everyone safe? Did you meet new friends? Did you do your best? How about when someone says something, that you are not sure how to take? When people say things with sarcasm, sometimes it's hurtful, but don't let it get you down. Always look for the good in the situation. Don't miss the opportunity to find the good in yourself and the other person.

Amos 5:14 "Seek good, not evil, that you may live. Then the Lord God Almighty will be with you, just as you say He is."

February 3

Do What Is Right

"But she started it." "But he wasn't being very nice first." Have you ever said something like this? We get wrapped up in other's thoughts, actions and behaviors. We shouldn't follow the lead on these types of behaviors, though. We should do what is right. God wants us to be more Christlike, to be without sin. Don't get wrapped up following a trail of negativity. Pray for His strength and guidance and follow Him instead.

2 Kings 17:15 "...Do not do as they do..."

1 John 2:6 (ESV) "Whoever says He abides in Him ought to walk in the same way in which He walked."

February 4

Trust in Him

A friend of mine once wrote this in an e-mail, "I'm so thankful that God doesn't tell us to understand...only to trust in Him." Isn't that so true? There will be many times, when we will not understand why things happened the way they did. You may want to question it or complain about it, but don't. Ask God to help you be okay with His plan. Tell Him you want to trust in Him. When you put your trust in Him completely and don't question it, you'll be amazed at how God will bless you through it all.

Proverbs 3:5 "Trust in the Lord with all your heart, and lean not on your own understanding."

February 5

"Those Who Enjoy Life, Will Live Forever"

Quoted by Anna Ray, February 2010

When we confess our sins and our belief in God, our lives are changed. You still have to work at it, but your life can be a wonderful experience. Putting your faith and trust in God, is a powerful thing. The Holy Spirit will live in you and help guide you. He will bring you to your happiest moments and carry you through your toughest times. The Holy Spirit will help you share what you know with others. God wants you (us) to live a happy life...with Him...forever!

Matthew 28:19-20 "Therefore go and make disciples of all nations, baptizing them in the name of the Father, the son and the Holy Spirit, and teaching them to obey everything I have commanded you. And surely I am with you always to the very end of the age."

February 6

You Can Always Count on Him

Throughout your life, you will have many friends. Those friends will have friends and some of them will become your friends. You'll really have a likeness for some people, but you may have a hard time getting along with others. God wants you to love each other. When you do, you will have the greatest friend of all...Him! Pray to God and ask Him to be with you during times when there are differences among you and your friends. He wants to help you. That's what friends are for!

John 15:12 "My Command is this: Love each other as I have loved you."

John 15:14 "You are my friends if you do as I command."

February 7 (Part 1)

Your Will Be Done

If you've ever prayed for something and not quite gotten the answer you would like, do not get discouraged. God knows your heart and sometimes, it might seem like He's not answering your prayers, but He is. He's answering with what is best for you. He loves you and cares for you. He knows your needs better than you do. Continue to pray, remembering to ask for peace and contentment, no matter what His will is for you.

Matthew 6:8 "...for your Father knows what you need before you ask Him."

February 8 (Part 2)

This Is How You Should Pray

Matthew 6:9-13 "This, then is how you should pray. 'Our Father in heaven, hallowed be your name, your kingdom come, your will be done on earth as it is in heaven. Give us today our daily bread. Forgive us our debts, as we also have forgiven our debtors. And lead us not into temptation, but deliver us from the evil one.'"

Keep it simple, get right to the point. Using the Lord's Prayer as a guide, talk to God as you would your best friend. Thank Him for what you have and for the protection He provides for you daily.

Matthew 6:6 "Then your Father who sees what is done in secret, will reward you."

February 9 (Part 1)

Think Before You Speak

Try this for fun! Hold your tongue and say "think before you speak." It's hard to tell what you are saying, isn't it? Sometimes we speak too quickly, or let our anger take over. It's hard to take back what you say, once you have said it. It's better to think before you speak, than to have to go back and apologize later, for something you shouldn't have said. Ask God to help you speak kind and gentle words in every situation. Ask Him to help you think before you speak.

Proverbs 10:19 "When words are many, sin is not absent, but he who holds his tongue is wise."

Proverbs 15:2 "The tongue of the wise commends knowledge, but the mouth of the fool gushes folly."

February 10 (Part 2)

Put Out the Fire

With our tongues we say so many things. We give praise, we compliment and we say words like love and admire. On the other hand, we are known for using our tongues to spread gossip, yell and even tell lies. It's hard to believe all of these can come from the same tongue, but it's true. Ask God to give you the words to speak. Ask Him to help you speak kindly to everyone, in all situations. Ask Him to help you put out the fire.

James 3:6 "The tongue also is a fire..."

James 3:9 "With the tongue we praise our Lord and Father, and with it we curse men, who have been made in God's likeness."

February 11

Tell Your Friends About Jesus

There are many ways we talk to our friends and many things we talk about. Your friends want to know about you, what you like and what you dislike. Tell your friends things about you by speaking to them in a kind and gentle way. Let them know your beliefs and most of all, tell them where you get your courage. Tell them about your friend, Jesus! Let them know what Jesus has done for you, what He has done for all of us.

Luke 8:39 "Return home and tell how much God has done for you."

John 4:41 "And many more believed because of His word."

February 12

Read God's Word Daily

We can grow closer to God by reading and studying His word daily. God wants us to get to know Him better. He gave us the bible so we could do that. Growing in God's word, helps us to gain knowledge of how we should live. It also helps us learn right from wrong, so we can "distinguish good from evil."

Hebrews 4:12 "For the word of God is alive and active. Sharper than any double-edged sword, it penetrates even to dividing soul and spirit, joints and marrow; it judges the thoughts and attitudes of the heart."

Hebrews 5:14 "...who by constant use have trained themselves to distinguish good from evil."

February 13

You Don't Have to Do It by Yourself

You will probably have situations in your life, when you'll wonder how you'll ever get through them. You may feel all alone, like no one understands or that nothing will help. When I was younger, I used to think that I should be able to fix things by myself. I often kept things to myself and decided they were private. The fact is, we all need God! We all need to come to Him in prayer. Sharing your pain with others will help you. The more people that know about your needs, the more you will be prayed for.

James 5:16 "Therefore confess your sins to each other and pray for each other so that you may be healed."

February 14

Do Everything in Love

Love...God created everything with love. He sent His son here for us because of love. Jesus died on the cross for our sins because He loves us. As you go through each day, each motion, do it with love in your heart. Do it to repay the love you've been shown. Do it with the love you've been taught. Love each other and love yourself. Be thankful to God for the love He allows in our lives and the love that He shows us. Most of all, love the idea of love.

Lamentations 3:22 "The faithful love of the Lord never ends!"

1 Corinthians 16:14 "Do everything in love."

February 15

Show Kindness to Others

You should always watch what you say and speak kindly to others. You can also show them you care, by your actions. By serving and being honest with everyone, they will know that you care about them. You can serve by helping around the house, by doing chores without being asked and by giving your all, in the work that you do. There are also a lot of ways you can get involved at your church. By choosing to be kind and serving in this way, you are not only showing them how much you care, you are setting an example for others.

1 John 3:18 "Dear children, let us not love with words or tongue but with actions and in truth."

February 16

Put God's Word into Practice

As we grow in our knowledge of God, by reading and studying His word, it will become easier and easier to make better choices. Just like with sports or homework, we get better when we study and practice. Take time to put God's word into practice, so that you can feel better about who you are and learn more about who God wants you to be.

Matthew 7:24 "Therefore everyone who hears these words of mine and puts them into practice is like a wise man who built his house on the rock."

Matthew 7:26 "But everyone who hears these words of mine and does not put them into practice is like a foolish man who built his house on sand."

February 17

Believe in Yourself

There will be times when you won't want to do something because you'll be afraid of making a mistake. Speaking in front of others or even going to camp or on a mission trip might be scary to you. Knowing God is with you is the best feeling you can have. Ask God to help you feel His presence. Ask Him to be with you during these times of uncertainty. Ask Him to help you feel better about making a mistake or not saying the right thing at the right time. We all make mistakes, so even if you do make one, know that God loves you and is with you. He wants you to be yourself and He wants you to come to Him. Don't be too proud to ask Him for help. He can help you increase your confidence, so that you can believe in yourself.

James 4:6 "God opposes the proud but gives grace to the humble."

James 4:10 "Humble yourselves before the Lord and He will lift you up."

February 18

Believe in Him

"Those who believe God is true, will always be true"
Quoted by Anna Ray, February 2010

Be true to yourself and to God. God wants you to believe in Him. When you believe in Him and put your faith in Him, it will be easier to get through tough situations. Knowing God and asking Him to comfort you and to be with you when you are struggling, is a wonderful feeling. God can help give you the hope you need and the confidence to share His good news with others.

John 3:17 "For God did not send His son into the world to condemn the world but to save the world through Him."

John 3:18 "Whoever believes in Him is not condemned, but whoever does not believe stands condemned already because He has not believed in the name of God's one and only son."

February 19

Confess Your Sins and Live

God did a wonderful thing for you and for me. He loves us so much! He sent His son to earth to give us such wonderful news. Jesus shared many stories with many people, so that we could know about Heaven. When Jesus died for us on the cross, He gave us an opportunity to be forgiven for our sins, so we could live with Him in Heaven forever. Confess your sins and let God know you are ready to answer His gift with a gift of your own...the gift of believing in Him...the gift of eternal life.

John 3:16 "For God so loved the world that He gave His one and only son, that whoever believes in Him shall not perish but have eternal life."

February 20

Share the Good News

It is a wonderful feeling being forgiven for your sins and accepting the Holy Spirit. It is a great thing knowing you never have to be alone. Don't you want to tell others how you feel? Don't you want everyone you know, to have the hope and love for our Father, that you now have? God wants you to share His good news.

Mark 16:15 "He said to them, 'Go into all the world and preach the good news to all creations.'"

Mark 16:20 "Then the disciples went out and preached everywhere with them and confirmed His word by the signs that accompanied."

February 21

Have His Word in Your Heart

By increasing your knowledge of Jesus and as your relationship with Him grows, you will become more and more aware of right and wrong. Daily reading of the bible will help you draw near and stay close to God. As you grow spiritually, you will want to say and do the right things. You will want to say and do things that are pleasing to others, but most of all, pleasing to God. Have His word in your heart!

Psalms 119:11 "I have hidden your word in my heart that I might not sin against you."

February 22

Be Thankful

Think about how wonderful it is, that God knows us so much, He answers our prayers before we even speak them. Sometimes we do not even know we are looking for or needing something and yet He gives it to us, at just the right time. When I think of all that God has given us, it makes me thankful beyond words. Thinking of Jesus Christ and what He did for us, so that we could have eternal life is so incredibly awesome! God continues to show us new things and new ways each and every day. Thank you, God, for loving us so much and helping us to remember the sacrifice you made, for each one of us.

Philippians 1:3 "I thank my God every time I remember you."

February 23

It Is More Blessed to Give

Being able to give is a wonderful feeling. Sometimes you may feel like you can't give because you don't have the time or the money. Ask God to help you be able to give. You can give material things you don't need anymore, by passing them along to the needy. You can give of your time, by helping in your local food pantry. Giving doesn't have to be about a huge amount of time or money. Give what you can, when you can and thank God for each opportunity to help.

Acts 20:35 "In everything I did, I showed you that by this kind of hard work we must help the weak, remembering the words the Lord Jesus himself said 'It is more blessed to give than to receive.'"

February 24

Listen & Obey

The wisest thing you could ever do, is listen to advice from your elders, especially your parents. I know it will be hard sometimes because you may want to follow your friends or make your own choices. Remember, even at this age your parents have been there. They are only trying to help you and they love you more than anything. Your Father, our God, sent Jesus to walk in our land to know what it was like to be human. Imagine Jesus knowing what it was like, to get advice and follow in His parent's footsteps.

Proverbs 19:20 "Listen to advice and accept instruction, and in the end you will be wise."

February 25

Repay Him with Your Service

Whatever you do, however you do it, do it for Him. God doesn't expect you to do things perfectly, but He knows you can do it. All He wants you to do, is to give it your best. No matter what it is, thank Him for the opportunity you were given and focus on Him the whole way. Don't get discouraged if it wasn't what you had in mind. I'm sure it's exactly what God wants you to be doing. If you keep the focus on Him and Him only, you'll be amazed at how blessed you will be.

Luke 4:8 "Worship the Lord your God and serve Him only."

February 26

Obey God's Word

As important as it is to read and study God's word, it is just as important, if not more, to obey His word. By obeying God's word, we are living how God wants us to live. He wants us to truly hear His heart and put it into practice. Our behavior and actions are contagious. If we can live a life with no sin, spreading our good attitude to others, just think how blessed we will all be, including the One that truly matters most.

Luke 11:28 "He replied; Blessed rather are those who hear the word of God and obey it."

February 27

Answer Gently

There have been times in my life when people have said things that were upsetting to me. Also, though I have been on the other end of it, where I have been the one that said the unkind words. Sometimes I have realized right away and even been able to tell them I was sorry. Unfortunately, though, there have also been times when I didn't realize what I said was hurtful. Maybe that has happened to you. Either you have been hurt or you have hurt someone else and didn't realize it. When we have God's word in our heart, we can be more aware of how we sound and be able to speak kinder words to those around us.

Proverbs 15:1 "A gentle answer turns away wrath, but a harsh word stirs up anger."

February 28

You Can Do It

I've made excuses in my life. I'm sure you have too. Whether you said, "I can't do it because I am too tired" or "I can't do it because I'm not good enough." God doesn't want us to make excuses. He wants to help us succeed in whatever it is we set our hearts and minds to. There will be times when God wants you to step out of your comfort zone and follow Him...You can do it!

Luke 14:18 "But they all alike began to make excuses."

2 Corinthians 9:8 "And God is able to make all grace abound to you, so that in all things at all times, having all that you need, you will abound in every good work."

February 29

Thank You God

All creatures big and small;

The mountains, lakes and everything tall.

God created them for us to enjoy,

Watching us take care of them is His joy.

Thank you, God, for all you've done.

Thank you for this earth and especially your Son.

Acts 4:24 "...you made the heavens and the earth
and the sea, and everything in them."

March 1

Don't Be Tempted by Negativity

Some days it is hard to have a positive attitude. Maybe you woke up late, your car won't start or you're running late for an appointment. It's through these times that you need to focus on God even more. Ask God to help you see the positive in the situation. Maybe He didn't want you to be in the wrong place at the wrong time. By running late, He put you just where He wanted you. Pray to God, so negative thoughts won't tempt you. Pray, so that you can have a more positive outlook, no matter how your day started.

Matthew 26:41 "Watch and pray so that you will not fall into temptation. The spirit is willing, but the body is weak."

March 2

There Are Some Things We Shouldn't Say

"I can't believe they acted that way." "I can't believe they did that." "I would never do that!" These are things we should never say about each other. Why? Because we all have faults, they are just not all the same. If you feel someone has done wrong, pray for them. Pray for God to reach out to them. We should always pray and lift each other up, not tear each other down.

Galatians 6:2 "Carry each other's burdens, and in this way you will fulfill the law of Christ."

March 3

Be Gracious to Everyone

You should always keep a good relationship with those around you. If you ever question your relationship with someone, talk to them. Keeping the communication open, lets people know the good in you. Don't be quick to judge what others are thinking. If you aren't sure how to handle a relationship you are currently in, ask God to help you understand it. Ask Him to help you be gracious to everyone, in every situation.

Proverbs 22:11 "He who loves a pure heart and whose speech is gracious will have the king for his friend."

March 4

Always Be Truthful

Don't get into a habit of lying to anyone. By being truthful to others, you can be true to yourself. You may think you are keeping yourself out of trouble, but all you are doing is making matters worse. If you lie, your friends won't trust you, and how about your parents or your boss? Wouldn't you rather be honest and keep your heart clear of lies? God wants you to be true to others, so you can continue to be true to yourself.

Proverbs 12:22 "The Lord detests lying lips, but He delights in men who are truthful."

March 5

God Likes Being Close to You

If you ever feel distant from the Lord, pray to Him. God likes being close to you. He wants to hear from you. If you haven't yet asked Him to come into your life, what better time than right now? You can be forgiven for your sins and can work toward being a better person. There is a place for you with Him. Don't wait any longer! Ask God to give you the confidence to come to Him and admit you need to be forgiven.

Acts 2:38-39 "Repent and be baptized, every one of you, in the name of Jesus Christ for the forgiveness of your sins. And you will receive the gift of the Holy Spirit. The promise is for you and your children and for all who are far off, for all whom the Lord our God will call."

March 6

Don't Say Anything You'll Regret

We will have many conversations in our lives. Most will be pleasant, but some may be strained. We might even want to let the other person know, that we think, what they said was wrong. Doing that might be easy, but is it the right thing to do? Try holding back from saying anything that may cause the relationship to be strained. Don't say anything that you will regret.

Proverbs 12:23 "A prudent man keeps his knowledge to himself, but the heart of fools blurts out folly."

March 7

God Knows Your Heart and Theirs

During our lives, we will see a lot of wonderful things. Also, though, there will be hardships that will take place. Watching the news or hearing the news of such things, may make you question "why do these things happen," or "why doesn't justice come to those who are at fault?" Trust the Lord to answer these questions and to hold the guilty accountable for what they have done. God knows your heart and theirs. Pray to Him for the peace you need in any situation. Ask Him for the courage to make a difference, in even just one person's life.

Proverbs 11:21 "Be sure of this: The wicked will not go unpunished, but those who are righteous will go free."

March 8

Attend Church & Get Involved

There have been times in my life when I felt like I wasn't good enough to get involved at church. The truth is, no one needs God more than those of us who think we aren't good enough. We are all sinners! By repenting and submitting ourselves to God, we are taking the first step toward making our lives better. We all need to be better; there is no one who needs God more than a sinner. Let God know you are ready. Let Him know you want to get involved in whatever way He wants you to. Let Him know you want to be a better person.

Mark 2:17 "...It is not the healthy who need a doctor, but the sick. I have not come to call the righteous, but sinners."

March 9

Great Is Your Reward in Heaven

"What about me," "When will it be my turn to shine," "Why was I overlooked?" Maybe you have asked similar questions and you have wondered why you have been overlooked so often. Remember, though, our time on earth is short and our reward will not come to us here. God wants you to live a life following Him. He wants you to look forward to your time in Heaven. Until then, trust in Him to know what is best for you. You may have been passed by or you haven't gotten what you think you deserve, but one day, you will rejoice with Him...the greatest reward of all!

Luke 6:23 "Rejoice in that day and leap for joy, because great is your reward in heaven."

March 10

Sticks and Stones May Break My Bones

Written by Susan Ray & Jimmy Ray

Maybe you have been hurt by someone's words, but remember, God loves you! God made you to be just the way you are. If you are feeling down about something, that someone said or did, don't look to man for comfort. Ask God to help you see the good in yourself and others. Ask Him to help you see them in a different light. Ask Him to help you both speak kinder to each other. God can help you, whenever you are hurt by someone else's words.

Psalms 34:20 "He protects all his bones, not one of them will be broken."

Proverbs 12:18 "There is one whose rash words are like sword thrusts, but the tongue of the wise brings healing."

March 11

Let Him Guide You

When you're feeling lost and you just don't know which way to go, let God be your guide. Someone once mentioned that they use the "2 by 4" prayer when they are seeking God's guidance. In other words, don't just pray about it, but pray and ask God to make it obvious, to make it very clear what direction you should take. Ask specifically for what you want and pray that it will come to you, as clear as if you were hit by a "2 by 4."

Psalm 120:1 "I call on the Lord in my distress and He answers me."

Isaiah 58:11 "The Lord will guide you always..."

March 12

Share What You Have Learned with Others

God wants you to be knowledgeable of Him, for so many reasons. Knowing Him will help you see the good in yourself and others. The more you know Him, the more you'll be able to trust in Him. You'll also have more faith and want to stay focused on His word. Most of all, the more you know Him, the more you will want to share what you have learned.

Isaiah 61:1 "The spirit of the sovereign Lord is on me, because the Lord has anointed me to preach good news to the poor…"

March 13

A Mother's Work Is Never Done

Mothers have many jobs, really both parents do! I could not list all the jobs here, even if I tried. However, I can tell you that as a mother of two, top on my list is caring for and loving my children. I have always wanted the best for them, but I admit, sometimes it's been hard. No matter what though, I have loved them unconditionally. God also wants the best for us. He wants us to love our children as He does. When you feel tired, remember God's promises. Remember that He promises to love us forever and He too, loves us unconditionally.

Proverbs 31:31 "Give her the reward she has earned, and let her works bring her praise at the city gate."

March 14

Love One Another

No matter what, be kind to others. If you think about it, we were all placed here for a reason. We are all just trying to live this life the best we know how. We walk through life, not always understanding each other. We can ask God to help us though. Pray to Him if you get irritated easily by the way someone else is acting towards you. We are all just trying to do our best. Try loving them and enjoy being loved in return.

Galatians 5:13 "You, my brothers, were called to be free. But do not use your freedom to indulge the sinful nature, rather, serve one another in love."

March 15

A Different Point of View

Just because you see things in a different way, than someone else, doesn't mean you are right and they are wrong. It also does not mean they are right. It just means you see things differently. It's okay to have your own opinion, just remember to be respectful when someone else has a different view than yours. Perhaps you should talk about it with them. Share your thoughts, but do it respectfully. Listen to their side and be open to changing your thoughts, if needed. Ask God to help you keep an open opinion in all areas whenever you have a different point of view.

Ephesians 4:3 "Make every effort to keep the unity of the spirit through the bond of peace."

March 16

Pass It On

Don't just share God's good news, live the good news. Of course, you should find ways to share it, though, too. Talk to others about the good things that have happened to you. Treat others with kindness, so they will want to know where you get your loving heart and kind ways. We do not know when Jesus will return, we only know that He will return. Pray for those that don't know Jesus. Pray for hearts that need to be changed. Pray for all to come forward and repent, so they can have the good news in their heart, to pass on to others as well.

Matthew 24:42 "Therefore keep watch, because you do not know on what day your Lord will come."

March 17

Encourage Them While You Raise Them Up

As a parent, I worry about my kids. There's probably a part of all of us, that can't help but worry about someone, at some point in our lives. When we raise our children with dignity and respect, we should feel good about trusting them because we have trusted Him. When they grow up and do more and more things independently, you will more than likely worry. You can't be there with them every minute of every day, but there is someone that can be. Pray to God as you let them go. Ask Him to come into their hearts and their lives. As they go out on their own, always remember they are not alone, so there is no need to worry.

Proverbs 22:6 "Train a child in the way he should go and when he is old he will not turn from it."

March 18

Stay Strong in the Lord's Word

No matter what, stay strong in the Lord's word. When you are knowledgeable of God's word, you can stay true to yourself and you can stay true to Him. Find time to read and meditate on His word daily. By doing this, you can show others how wonderful it is to know Him. If they have a sinful nature, you can help show them a better way, a more positive manner in which to behave. Know God's word, study His word and live God's word.

Proverbs 23:12 "Apply your heart to instruction and your ears to words of knowledge."

March 19

Friends Will Come and Friends May Go

You will have many friends throughout your life. Some friends will be in your life for a reason. They may be brought to you by God, possibly during a rough time in your life. Some may only be in your life for a season. These friends may also be there, for only a short time, but are most likely sent to you for one reason or another. No matter the relationship or the reason, pray for your friends. Pray that you will be a good friend to them, no matter how long they are in your life.

Proverbs 17:17 "A friend loves at all times."

Proverbs 27:9 "A sweet friendship refreshes the soul."

March 20 (Part 1)

Ask and You Shall Receive

Whenever you feel tired and need rest, ask God to give you rest. Whenever you feel lost and afraid, ask for courage. If you ever feel alone, ask God to help you feel His presence. Whenever you do not know how to pray, ask for God's wisdom. In anything and everything...seek Him!

Matthew 7:7 "Ask and it will be given to you; seek and you will find; knock and the door will be opened."

Matthew 7:8 "For everyone who asks receives; he who seeks finds; and to him who knocks, the door will be opened."

March 21 (Part 2)

He Will Give You Rest

I have had some days, where I have been so tired, I did not know how I would ever keep going. Then there are some days, when I've been so busy, I really haven't known where to start or when to stop. I've wanted to be able to get everything done, but I've also wanted to be able to do it myself. No one is expecting you to be able to do it all. It's okay to ask for help. It's also okay to let it all go. More than anything else, it's okay to rest. Take care of yourself and through it all, ask God to allow you time for rest.

Matthew 11:28 "Come to me, all you who are weary and burdened, and I will give you rest."

March 22

Wisdom Comes from the Holy Spirit

Once you have repented of your sins and accepted Christ as your Savior, you will be amazed at the power of the Holy Spirit. What a wonderful gift! God has allowed us to know Him, through the Spirit. Things you did before, may now be seen in a different light. Listen to the Spirit's wisdom, so you can recognize your sins. Ask God to help you grow, so you can become more and more Christlike, each and every day.

1 Corinthians 2:9-10 "...No eye has seen, no ear has heard, no mind has conceived what God has prepared for those who love Him, but God has revealed it to us by His spirit."

March 23

There is Nothing You Can't Do

I've had days and times in my life, when no matter what I did, I felt as if I was doing the wrong thing. I've also said words that came out wrong or at the wrong time. It made me feel like giving up! When you have days like that, turn to God. Ask Him to give you the courage to keep going, the strength you need to finish. He will fill you with hope because of His love for you. When you have that hope within you, there is nothing you can't do.

2 Corinthians 4:8-9 "We are hard pressed on every side, but not crushed; perplexed, but not in despair; persecuted, but not abandoned; struck down, but not destroyed."

March 24

How Can You Tell Others About God?

There are many ways we communicate with each other. We have many things to share. How will you share God's news? God made us all different. He also made our interests and talents different as well. I've always enjoyed writing and working with kids. I can look back and see how God has led me to write, as well as teach Sunday school, lead small groups and much more. It is no mistake that God placed me here to share His news. What way can you tell others about God? How has God blessed you? Look for the signs, listen and then tell others.

Mark 16:20 "Then the disciples went out and preached everywhere, and the Lord worked with them and confirmed His word by the signs that accompanied it."

March 25

We've All Been There

We've all been there...a stressful day, the loss of a loved one, the loss of a job or just not feeling well. Yes, there will be trials in our lives, but these trials will make us stronger. It is through these times, that we need to turn to God. We will learn to pray harder and turn our focus on Him. We need Him during these times, more than any other times in our lives. When we understand that and turn to Him, for strength and comfort, He will see us through. Turn to Him and see what a blessing it is, to come through your trials stronger than you were before.

James 1:2-3 "Consider it pure joy, my brother, whenever you face trials of many kinds because you know that the testing of your faith develops perseverance."

March 26

Reflect on Jesus

My favorite part of Spring is hearing the birds chirp early in the morning. To me, it's a reminder of not only the beauty that God created, but the living things around us. As the weather warms up and flowers bloom, we are reminded of the renewed spirit within us. Jesus died on the cross, so we could be forgiven for our sins. He was brought back to life, so we can see the hope of eternal life. If we accept His gift and believe, we too can bloom again and again and be reminded of the constant change in us. Spring is a wonderful time to reflect on Jesus...what He did for us, by dying on the cross and allowing us to have the hope of eternal life.

Luke 24:46-47 "He told them, 'This is what is written: The Christ will suffer and rise from the dead on the third day, and repentance and forgiveness of sins will be preached in His name to all nations, beginning at Jerusalem."

March 27

How Amazing He Is

It amazes and encourages me to know what Jesus did for us and the good news He brought with Him. The wonderful way He was able to live His life, so loving and caring. Jesus lived a life without sin. He preached, He helped and He protected. Jesus did so many wonderful, powerful things, during His time on earth. The greatest of these was dying on the cross for us. The love, the courage and the sacrifice He showed is truly amazing!

John 21:25 "Jesus did many other things as well. If every one of them were written down, I suppose that even the whole world would not have room for the books that would be written."

March 28 (Part 1)

Trust God's Plan for You

I strongly believe there are no coincidences. God has a plan for us. Throughout your life, there may be days when you feel let down. Maybe something didn't go your way. Maybe you didn't get the job, that you thought for sure you'd get. Maybe someone told you about a job, that you never would have expected you'd find interest in. It's those times, that we should put our trust in God even more. He knows what you need and He wants you, to not only believe in Him, but to trust in Him completely. You'll be so happy you did!

Isaiah 25:9 "...This is the Lord, we trusted in Him; let us rejoice and be glad in His salvation."

March 29 (Part 2)

Don't Live Your Life Asking Why

God made you and this world, with good things in mind. He loves us and knows what's best. If something doesn't turn out like you'd like it to, don't get upset at the situation or the people that might have changed it. Don't pass judgment on something, that is out of your control...out of our control. We are all made for God's purpose. Ask Him to help you have peace in the moment, especially when you don't understand why something happened or didn't happen, the way you wanted it to.

Ecclesiastes 3:17 "I thought in my heart, God will bring to judgment both the righteous and the wicked, for there will be a time for every activity, a time for every deed."

March 30

Be Compassionate to Others

We should live life caring for and loving each other. We are all different, not one of us is the same. We all have the ability to show each other how good we are and how good God made us to be. God shows us compassion and loves us so much. Make a difference today in some else's life. Treat them with the love you are given by God. Treat them the way you want to be treated; the way God wants you to feel treated.

Psalms 145:8-9 "The Lord is gracious and compassionate, slow to anger and rich in love. The Lord is good to all; He has compassion on all He has made."

March 31

Take His Words to Heart

Sometimes, we are very hard on ourselves, taking things to heart and taking them personally. At times, someone might say something to you, that they meant one way and you take it another way. God loves you, no matter what! He wants you to love others too. If you are hurt by what they said, ask God to help you. God does not want you to worry about what others are saying. He doesn't want you to be discouraged by words, that weren't meant to hurt you. Turn to Him and ask Him to help you forgive and forget. The only words you should be taking to heart, are His words.

Psalm 119:11 "I have hidden your word in my heart that I might not sin against you."

95

April 1 (Part 1)

He Cares for You

You are reading this right now because someone cares about you. Someone cares enough about you, to tell you what Jesus has done for you. Jesus loves you so much, that He walked this earth for you. He understands everything you are going through. He went through more than any bad day you will ever go through. He did it with a positive attitude, which we can hope to one day have. He did not sin; He did not anger. He did God's will without question because He loves you so much. Jesus wants the best for you. He wants you to live each day, with an attitude like He had because He cares for you.

Psalms 33:20-21 "We wait in hope for the Lord; He is our help and our shield, in Him our hearts rejoice, for we trust in His holy name."

April 2 (Part 2)

Let Us Not Forget

When we set our eyes on Him and focus on what Jesus did for us, our lives will be so much more fulfilled. I pray that as you read this and go through this week, that you will reflect on, not only what Jesus did for us, but why He did it. Jesus paid the ultimate sacrifice because of His love for us. Think about that...His love for you! May we continue to ask God to help us do His will. As we set our eyes on Him, may we never forget Jesus' ultimate sacrifice.

Hebrews 13:20 "Now may the God of peace, who through the blood of the eternal covenant brought back from the dead our Lord Jesus, that great Shepherd of the sheep, equip you with everything good for doing His will, and may He work in us what is pleasing to Him, through Jesus Christ, to whom be glory for ever and ever. Amen."

April 3

This World Is Only Temporary

As we go through each day, we need to remember that we are living in a world, that is only a temporary home. Eventually, we will go to a wonderful place and be re-united with our creator.

'God, help us to remember, that we are only here for a short time. Help us to not get too attached to things of this world, that do not matter. Help us to keep our focus on what truly matters...doing your will until we can spend eternity with you. In Jesus's name, Amen!'

Psalm 119:19 (TEV) "I am here on earth for just a little while."

1 John 2:17 "The world and it's desires pass away, but the man who does the will of God lives forever."

April 4

Start Your Relationship with Jesus Christ Today

How do you spend your days? Do you read God's word daily? Do you make the most of your time? Are you trusting God to help guide your life? If not, it's not too late to start. It's never too late to turn to God. The best way to find out your purpose, is to start a relationship with Jesus. He wants you to pray to God in His name. Let God know you are ready to live a life following Him and doing His will. Let God know you are ready to have a close, personal relationship with Jesus Christ.

2 Peter 1:2 "Grace and peace be yours in abundance through the knowledge of God and of Jesus our Lord."

April 5

Unconditional Love

Our love for others should be real. We should do things for others out of love, so we can be pleasing to God. God knows your heart and He knows whether you are doing them out of love or because you feel like you have to. Pray to God and ask Him for unconditional love, so that you will love others, no matter what. Ask Him to show you how to love, so you do not envy others or get easily angered by someone. Love should be complete and without sin. You are capable of loving completely. Ask God to show you how.

1 Corinthians 13:4-7 "Love is patient, love is kind. It does not envy, it does not boast, it is not proud. It is not rude, it is not self-seeking, it is not easily angered, it keeps no record of wrongs. Love does not delight in evil but rejoices with the truth. It always protects, always trusts, always hopes, always perseveres."

April 6 (Part 1)

Use Your Talents to Serve Others

Don't be afraid to do something you have never done before. Whenever you are asked to do something, whether it is a special project, or volunteering at church, at school or at work, know that God believes in you. We were given many talents that God gave us to use. Even when you don't think you can do it; God knows you can. He wants you using your talents to serve others.

1 Peter 4:10 "Each one should use whatever gift you have received to serve others, faithfully administering God's grace in its various forms."

April 7 (Part 2)

A Servant's Heart

Whether you are serving your family, or serving a dinner at church, you should always serve with a giving heart. Serve openly and serve often, knowing you are doing exactly what God has made you to do. If you get tired, ask for strength. If you don't think you are qualified or you are afraid, ask for wisdom and courage. Most of all when you are done, give thanks. Be thankful for the opportunity God provided for you and entrusted you with. Give thanks for the ability to serve others with a servant's heart.

1 Peter 4:11 "…If anyone serves, he should do it with the strength God provides, so that in all things God may be praised through Jesus Christ…"

April 8

God is Calling You

There is no mistake that you are reading this. God wants you to receive this message. I believe God allowed my hand to put these words together, but they are His messages. It is clear to me, especially now, that God knows His children and knows them well. If you are being called to Him, answer His call. Don't wait any longer!

1 Peter 4:7 "The end of all things is near. Therefore, do not wait until it is too late, get to know Him now."

1 Peter 5:10 "And the God of all grace, who called you to His eternal glory in Christ, after you have suffered a little while, will himself restore you and make you strong, firm and steadfast."

April 9

The Lord Hears Those Who Call

The more I learn about God and the closer I get to Him, the more at peace I feel. There have been times in my life though, when I have become comfortable and not prayed as often as I should have. There have been many other times however, when I have prayed continually and intently. It's always in those times, when I have felt God's presence, His wisdom and His peace. Wherever you are in your spiritual journey, call out to Him, pray about everything, all the time. The Lord hears all who call out to Him.

Acts 2:21 "And everyone who calls on the name of the Lord will be saved."

April 10

Believing is Seeing

Jesus loves you so much and wants you to believe in Him. One day He will come back to this earth. He'll be ready to take you with Him to heaven, forever. If you believe, let someone know! Pray and ask God to give you the confidence to tell others that you believe and the courage to repent, so that you can be forgiven for your sins. By believing and repenting, one day, you too, will be able to see wonderful things that are not of this world, like Jesus.

1 John 5:1 "Everyone who believes that Jesus is the Christ is born of God, and everyone who loves the father loves his child as well."

1 John 5:4-5 "for everyone born of God overcomes the world...who is it that overcomes the world? Only he who believes that Jesus is the Son of God."

April 11

A Blessing in Itself

God's promise of heaven came with such a huge sacrifice, that we will never fully comprehend what all was done for us. That we can be forgiven for our sins, is such a special gift in itself. On top of that though, God has promised, that after this life, we can live with Him forever. What a blessing it is and what a true blessing it will be.

Hebrews 12:2 "Let us fix our eyes on Jesus, the author and perfecter of our faith, who for the joy set before Him endured the cross scorning its shame, and sat down at the right hand of the throne of God."

Acts 26:18 "… so that they may receive forgiveness of sins and a place among those who are sanctified by faith in me."

April 12

Teaching Others

If you get the chance to teach or tell others of Jesus' good news, do so, but do so carefully. Make sure you are able to speak confidently, so they can see and know about Jesus. God wants you to share this news and is pleased when you speak of Him to others. Before preparing for a Sunday school lesson or whenever I prepare for small group time, I always pray to God and ask Him to give me the words to speak. I want the words to be His and not mine. Ask Him to help you, so you can share His message confidently.

Hebrews 6:10 "God is not unjust; He will not forget your work and the love you have shown Him as you have helped His people and continue to help them."

April 13

Be a Good Listener

Be a good listener, and get all the facts. Sometimes we hear things and automatically assume we know all the information we need, in order to form an opinion. The truth is we don't know every thought the other person has or why they did or didn't do something a certain way. Always "be quick to listen," by showing others how interested you are in them and their thoughts. Be "slow to speak" and make sure you say the right thing, by choosing your words carefully. More importantly, be "slow to become angry." Keep your focus on God, His plan and His desires for you.

James 1:19-20 "My dear brothers, take note of this: Everyone should be quick to listen, slow to speak and slow to become angry, for man's anger does not bring about the righteous life that God desires."

April 14

Honesty is the Best Policy

Be honest in all things, always speaking the truth. When you are honest with your feelings and in your words, others will trust you more. You will have better relationships because of it. When your truthfulness is pleasing to others, think how much more pleasing it will be to God. He wants you to be truthful with everyone and with yourself. In doing so, He will rejoice with delight.

Proverbs 23:16 "my inmost being will rejoice when your lips speak what is right"

April 15

Stop and Think

Before you ever make a decision about how to react in a situation, stop and think. Perhaps you didn't like the way someone looked at you...you didn't realize they were really thinking about a family member who was sick. Maybe someone snapped at you...you didn't know they had just found out they lost their job. Remember, you can never fully know what someone else is thinking or going through. You can also never fully know what God has planned for you. Be patient and kind to everyone, knowing that God is in control. Remember that God wants you to trust in His plan, for you and for them.

John 13:7 "Jesus replied, 'You don't understand what I'm doing now, but someday you will.'"

April 16

Suffering Produces Perseverance

Sometimes it might seem impossible to understand, but suffering makes us stronger. During your times of hurt, you may not always see it right away, but God will bring you through it. He knows just what you need. You will not be disappointed, if you stay close to Him, through His word and through prayer.

Romans 5:3-5 "...we also rejoice in our sufferings, because we know that suffering produces perseverance, perseverance, character; and character, hope. And hope does not disappoint us, because God has poured out His love into our hearts by the Holy Spirit, whom He has given us."

April 17

The One and Only

In all your days, look to God. He is on your side. He wants you to do your very best in all things. Some days you may feel like everyone is out to get you, no one is listening to you, and no one is on your side. Turn to God! Ask Him to help you see others in a different way. Ask Him to help you find your way. Share your true feelings with God, pour it out to Him. He loves you so much; He is the one and only true God and protector.

2 Kings 17:39 "… worship the Lord your God; it is He who will deliver you from the hand of all your enemies."

April 18

Your Worship Should Be Pleasing to Him

There are many ways to worship. There are also many reasons why we worship. Just make sure that when you worship, your heart and your focus are on the right things. Don't worship as a show for others. Don't worship in a way that wouldn't be true to who you are. Worship to be pleasing to God. Worship in a way that lets Him know where your heart is. God will be so pleased with you and you will be so amazed, at how wonderful your true worship will feel.

Hebrews 12:28 (TEV) "Let us be grateful and worship God in a way that will please Him."

April 19

There is a Way

There is no better gift that you could ever receive, than knowing Jesus Christ died for your sins. Jesus entered this world in human form, so that He could relate with us. What's amazing to me, is that no matter what type of person or people He came up against, He never sinned. Isn't that wonderful? Don't you wish you could be just like Jesus? My prayer for us, is to not only believe in Him, but to want to be like Him. There is a way... Jesus is the way!

Romans 5:8 "... While we were still sinners, Christ died for us."

Romans 5:11 "Not only is this so, but we also rejoice in God through our Lord Jesus Christ, through whom we have now received reconciliation."

April 20

Plain and Simple

When you think about it, God really doesn't ask much from us. It's plain and simple actually. He wants us to do what is right. How do we do that you ask? Well, we seek Him, we get to Know Him, we fall in love with Him, and we follow Him. Somewhere during this journey, we learn to desire Him. When our hearts are true and the desire is there, we will want to do what is right. We will desire to do what is right.

Isaiah 1:16-17 "...Stop doing wrong, learn to do right."

April 21

Give Thanks for Everything

When we think about our times of trouble and our times of hurt, that is when we should turn to God even more. Yes, we will have difficult days, but none compare to the day Jesus gave His life for us. God wants us to know how much He loved us and still loves us today. We can focus on that day and on Jesus and be thankful for all He has done for us. When we thank God, through Jesus, He will know His death wasn't for nothing. That kind of love shows us even more, why we should be thankful for everything we have and everything we are able to get through.

Ephesians 5:20 "always giving thanks to God the Father for everything, in the name of our Lord Jesus Christ."

April 22 (Part 1)

Alike or Different, Love Them All

Remember what our focus on this earth is. God wants us to love ourselves and each other. Sometimes it will be hard to love someone who is different than you, but God created them too. None of us are perfect and we all need each other. They may not do something like you would, but does that make them any less than you? Ask God to help you be open to their way, their suggestions and their love. Ask Him to help you show them, the love you show Him.

Galatians 5:14 "Love your neighbor as yourself."

April 23 (Part 2)

Do Good to Everyone

What a wonderful feeling, when someone thinks to ask us how we are. It's nice to be thought of and it's great to know that we are loved. As you go through each day think of ways you can make someone's day. How can you show them, that they are loved and thought of today? A kind word or maybe a card to let them know someone is thinking of them and praying for them. Even a simple smile can make someone's day.

Galatians 6:10 "Therefore, as we have opportunity, let us do good to all people..."

April 24

Prayer Is So Wonderful

Remember, it is not only important to pray when you are by yourself, but you should also get involved some way, where you are able to pray with others. Be open with your prayer requests too, so that they can pray for you. Remember that God hears our prayers, especially when "2 or more come together" and pray. It is such an honor that we are able to come to God in prayer, in so many ways and for so many reasons.

Matthew 18:20 "For where two or three come together in my name, there am I with them."

April 25

Share God's News with Your Children

You should not only live by God's word; you should also share it with your children. Scripture says "talk about them (God's Commandments) when you sit...and when you walk..." I want God and His word to be my daily focus...continually. More importantly, I want my children to know and live by His word. I want to share with them what I know, so that they too, will have God's word in their heart.

Deuteronomy 6:6-9 "These commandments that I give you today are to be upon your ears. Impress them on your children. Talk about them when you sit at home and when you walk along the road, when you lie down and when you get up. Tie them as symbols on your hands and bind them on your foreheads. Write them on the door frames of your houses and on your gates."

April 26

Keep the Peace

I believe there are no mistakes and that things happen for a reason. Knowing this and remembering it are two different things. We truly need to remember this in order to stay peaceful with everyone and in all situations. If God meant it to be this way, who are we to question it? Why should we get upset about it? Keep the peace with everyone. Ask God to help you stay focused on His will, His plan, and His peace for you.

Romans 14:19 "Let us therefore make every effort to do what leads to peace..."

April 27

Becoming Christlike

Becoming Christlike is something you will work on your whole life. By allowing the Holy Spirit to help you see things with God's vision, it will be easier for you to change to become more Christlike. Listen often and listen intently to the whispers within you. Ask God to help you hear the Holy Spirit and be led down a better path. I'm not saying it will be easy, but if you stay focused on God, you will notice a change within yourself.

1 Corinthians 2:12 "We have not received the spirit of the world but the Spirit who is from God, that we may understand what God has freely given us."

April 28

Change Allows Growth

Sometimes change is scary. We get used to the way things are and then all of a sudden, we are told it will change. God doesn't want us to be scared to make changes. He wants us to be open to them. Think about how dull life would be if everything, every day was the same. By allowing change in our lives, it allows us to grow. We are able to grow because, not only do we learn a new way of doing something, but we learn to trust God. If you are going through changes in your life, pray for God to help you accept those changes. Pray that you will trust Him to know what's best.

Romans 12:2 "Do not conform any longer to the pattern of this world, but be transformed by the renewing of your mind. Then you will be able to test and approve what God's will is – His good, pleasing, and perfect will."

April 29

Stay Focused on Him to do His Will

Don't get too down when you are going through tough times. God doesn't intend for tough times to last forever. When you go through times of trouble, you learn to not only lean on others, but most of all, Him. Pray to God for His guidance through these times. Ask Him to help you see the good in all things. Ask Him to help you stay focused on Him, so you can do His will and do what is pleasing to Him. You'll come through better and stronger, not only as a person, but as a believer.

Romans 8:28 "And we know that in all things God works for the good of those who love Him, who have been called according to His purpose."

April 30

Let the Holy Spirit Speak to You

When you give yourself and your life to Jesus, you also accept the Holy Spirit in your life. The Holy Spirit will help guide you and lead you, if you'll listen. Trust those little "nudges" from within, that remind you of what is right and what is wrong. As you listen and obey, you will be less and less tempted to sin and more likely to be changed for the better. Stay focused on God and what is good and you will continue to become more Christlike.

Luke 8:18 "Therefore consider carefully how you listen."

1 Kings 19:12 "The Holy Spirit often nudges us with a gentle whisper."

May 1

We Cannot Fulfill His Purpose Alone

As believers, we are part of a family, a family of other believers. We cannot fulfill His purpose alone. It takes all of us, each with our own unique qualities. God intended it that way and its one of the reasons He made us all different. We each have our own gifts and because of this, we can fulfill His will for us and for each other, together.

1 Corinthians 12:4 "There are different kinds of gifts, but the same Spirit."

1 Corinthians 12:11 "All these are the work of one and the same Spirit."

May 2

Do Good to Others, No Matter What

Someone once wrote on their Facebook account, something about people being rude. They mentioned they didn't think they should open doors for anyone or do anything nice for others, if they didn't get a "thank you" for doing it. It really made me stop and think because I may have felt that way at one time or another. However, as a Christian, I have learned that we should still do these things for others, no matter what. Don't do them expecting to get a "thank you" or a "way to go." Do them to be helpful to others and pleasing to God. Do them as if you were doing them for God.

Ephesians 5:21 "Submit to one another out of reverence to Christ."

May 3

We All Have Bad Days

No one can possibly know everything you are going through or everything you have been through. The return of this is also true. You can not entirely know what others have been through or what they are going through. Because of this, you should not take things too personal if someone upsets you. They are human, just like you. They are sinners, just like you. They have good and bad days too. The best thing to do, for someone that has wronged you in some way, is to pray for them. Ask God to come into their lives. Ask Him to bless them, so they might be a blessing to others.

Luke 6:28 "bless those who curse you, pray for those who mistreat you."

May 4

Comfort Those in Need

There will be times in our lives, when someone will need us to be there for them. Just as others are there for us, in our times of need, we need to be there for them too. To truly do this, we need to stop what we're doing and really listen to them. Focus your attention on them, what their needs are and what they are saying. By comforting them when they need it, you can help others see the good in Him.

2 Corinthians "… who comforts us in all our troubles, so that we can comfort those in any trouble with the comfort we ourselves have received from God."

May 5

Your Troubles Won't Last

It's good to know that our troubles are not going to last. It's also good to know, that when we go through any amount of trouble in our lives, there is sometimes a reason behind it. Will we always know the reason? Probably not, but God knows what is best for us. Perhaps He's preparing you for something else down the road. Perhaps He wants you to grow in ways you didn't know you could. Usually, when you look back on your troubles, you'll realize they weren't that bad after all. I'm not saying you'll always see it that way, but most of the time, thankfully, they'll be "light and momentary."

2 Corinthians 4:17 "For our light and momentary troubles are achieving for us an external glory that far outweighs them all."

May 6

Become a Peacemaker

If you ever feel you've been wronged, you should keep the peace. You're not going to solve anything by getting angry or worse...getting even. Be the peaceful one, reflecting what God intends for all of us. Show love and compassion, in every situation. We're all living our lives the best we can. Let's keep it peaceful by showing others the mercy and grace, that God has shown us.

Proverbs 13:3 "He who guards his lips guards his life, but he who speaks rashly will come to ruin."

May 7

Practice What You Preach

Make sure you live each day with Christ in mind. Christ lived His life on earth sinless. He spread God's news of Heaven and showed many people the way to eternity. He was not always treated fairly and obviously, in the end of his time on earth, was treated unimaginable. During it all though, he remained a good example of what God wants from us. Make sure you live a life that you can be proud of. Spread God's good news with honor, in the same way Jesus Christ did. Don't we owe Him at least that, for all He did and does for us?

Philippians 1:27 "Whatever happens, conduct yourselves in a manner worthy of the gospel of Christ."

May 8

Praise Always

Isn't it much better to hear good things, rather than bad things about yourself?   Don't you feel better when you are saying good things about yourself and others? Saying and doing things that are pleasing to God, shows others how great it can be to follow Him. Remember, God made us all.   He wants us to be loving and kind to one another, through our actions and our words.

James 3:9 "With the tongue we praise our Lord and Father, and with it we curse men, who have been made in God's likeness."

James 3:10 "Out of the same mouth came praise and cursing. My brothers, this should not be."

May 9

Praise Him

There are so many things in our lives we should be thankful for. Even on a bad day, we can find something to be thankful for. Be thankful for the sunshine after a cloudy day. Look how the flowers bloomed after the rainy day. How about the wind, that helped dry up all that rain? God gives us so many things. Sometimes, we need to stop and look for the good, but it's always there. Praise God for all He has done and continues to do. He wants you to notice what He's done for you

Psalm 67:3 "May the peoples praise you, O God; may all the peoples praise you."

May 10

God Has Called You

God has called you to follow Him. When you repent and are forgiven for your sins, your life starts changing. The Holy Spirit can help guide you, but you need to do your part too. Listen to the Holy Spirit. Read and learn God's word, so that you will know how to live. God wants you to be aware of how you're living. He wants you to allow change in your life. He wants you to follow Him!

1 Peter 2:1 "...Therefore, rid yourselves of all malice and all deceit, hypocrisy, envy, and slander of every kind."

May 11

How Can We Stop Sinning?

So many of us do things over and over again, knowing it is wrong. Why do we do it? How can we stop sinning? God wants to help you. He wants you to be the person He created you to be. Get to know God! Let Him know you believe in Him and that you believe in Jesus. Are you ready to start doing what's right? Good! Let someone know! Repent to God and be forgiven for your sins. He is not only ready for you, He is waiting!

John 3:36 "Whoever believes in the Son has eternal life, but whoever rejects the Son will not see life, for God's wrath remains on him."

May 12

God Sent You to Earth for a Reason

As you learn more and more about God and really get to know Him, you will be so in love with Him. You'll realize God sent you to earth for a reason. He'll put you where He wants you, when He wants you there. At times, you'll know He's right there with you. At other times, you may not feel Him there, but when you look back on the situation, you'll know He never left you. Everything you do should be for God's pleasure. He sent you here to do His will. He sent you here for a reason.

John 5:30 "...for I seek not to please myself but Him who sent me."

May 13

Do It for the Right Reason

Think about it, one day we will be serving God! You should feel honored to know, that He wants you serving Him. He is looking forward to that day even more than you are because He knows it will be pleasing to you too. You don't have to wait to serve God until you get to Heaven. Start now! Everything you do, you should be doing as if you are serving Him. Don't do it for the glory or the honor or the thanks you'll get, or not get, here on earth. Do it for the right reason, the one and only reason...your one true Father. Serve Him only!

2 Corinthians 10:18 "For it is not the one who commands himself who is approved, but the one whom the Lord commands."

May 14

No Two Are Alike

Have you ever been in a position where you thought that you were working harder than someone else or thought they weren't working hard enough? By doing that, not only are you taking the focus off of the work you are doing, you are also taking your eye off of Him. I have learned that no two are alike! We are able to work together because of this. We shouldn't knock each other down, we should lift each other up...not by comparing ourselves, but by focusing on what really matters most...God!

Galatians 5:26 (Msg) "We will not compare ourselves with each other as if one of us were better and another worse. We have far more interesting things to do with our lives. Each of us is an original."

May 15

See a Little Clearer

As I grow in my knowledge of Christ and my relationship with Him grows, I feel like I am able to see things differently. Since knowing Him, there have been times that I have wronged others. When I've done this, I have seen where I've hurt them. Sometimes, it has come back to hurt me in some way too. I was able to see, that by doing wrong in the first place it started a domino effect. Does this mean my relationship with Him will help me stop sinning? Probably not completely, but I do believe it does mean I will sin less. Stay focused on Him and you'll see clearer too.

Psalm 119:71 "It was good for me to be afflicted so that I might learn your decrees."

May 16

Share His News

God has done so many wonderful things in my life. It is hard for me not to share this good news with others. I have been blessed to be able to share His news and I pray these things for you too. In whatever way you can think of, share His news. It could be in a kind word, a good deed or a kind gesture, showing your love for Him. Maybe God has invited you to share His news by leading or teaching. Whatever it is, go for it! Ask God to give you the words to speak and the confidence to share His news.

Psalm 121:1-2 "...where does my help come from? My help comes from the Lord, the Maker of heaven and earth."

May 17

Do Not Give in To Them

It seems that most of my life, I was always trying to do things on my own. I didn't want to listen to words of wisdom from older siblings or even my own parents. Most of us are that way; we have to learn from our own mistakes. We know right from wrong at an early age. Thankfully, we know that it doesn't make sense to do some things. Ask God to help you stay on that road. Don't give in to sin!

Proverbs 1:10 "My son, if sinners entice you, do not give in to them."

May 18

You Might Be Surprised

Don't just share God's news where you are. Ask God if He wants you traveling the world to share His news. You might be surprised what you are capable of doing. God made you and knows exactly what you are able to do. Even if you think "that's not for me" or "I couldn't do that," listen to God. He might be telling you, that He knows you can and He wants you to. Believe in yourself, trust in Him!

Colossians 1:6 "...All over the world this gospel is bearing fruit and growing, just as it has been doing among you since the day you heard it and understood God's grace in all its truth."

May 19

Make the Decision Your Heart Longs For

If you are waiting to make the decision to accept Jesus Christ as your Savior, pray God will give you the confidence you need to do it. Pray every day until it happens. Don't wait until it is too late to make the decision. Don't put it off any longer! God loves you and wants you to come to Him. One day soon this world will change as we know it. Isn't it time you made the decision your heart is longing for?

Isaiah 13:6 "...for the day of the Lord is near..."

May 20

Pray More, Worry Less

Before my relationship with Jesus I worried about many things. I worried so much sometimes that I couldn't sleep. I also missed out on doing some things because I was too worried to try something new. Jesus has led me down a different path. I know I can turn to Him in my time of worry. I feel like a weight has been lifted because I know that, through prayer, I can be relieved of some of my worry. I truly do worry less because I pray more and prayer has made all the difference.

Proverbs 12:25 "An anxious heart weighs a man down, but a kind word cheers him up."

May 21

Live Better and Feel Better

When you live a righteous life, you really do feel better about yourself and your relationship with Jesus. There is nothing better than knowing, that God is on your side. Feeling that inner-peace, makes you feel so good about so many things. Not only do you feel good inside, but when others see you at peace, it makes them feel good as well.

Proverbs 16:7 "When a man's ways are pleasing to the Lord, he makes even his enemies live at peace with him."

May 22

Don't Get Discouraged, Let God Lead You

Don't get discouraged, let God lead your steps. Remember, God has a plan for you and if something doesn't go how you thought it would, it's probably because it's not part of His plan. When this happens to me, I try to look at it as a blessing instead of a disappointment. Think of it like this...God is using you in His plan, how awesome is that!

Proverbs 16:9 "In his heart a man plans his course, but the Lord determines his steps."

May 23

God Is in Control of All Your Days

It's easy to be happy when things are going well. What about when you're not having a great day? How do you react when your day doesn't go as you would like it to? As a Christian, it's important to keep your focus on the Lord. However, as human beings, it is easy to get lost in our own thoughts and feelings. As you grow in your relationship with Him, you'll be so glad that God is in control of all your days.

Ecclesiastes 7:14 "When times are good, be happy; but when times are bad, consider: God has made the one as well as the other."

May 24

God's Light Will Shine

God wants us to tell everyone we know about Him. I know you might be asking how you can do this. You might even think that it's not possible. It is possible, though and there are many ways to do it. Sometimes, just acting on a feeling is the only thing you need. You might have thought about sending a card to brighten someone's day or what about getting the door for someone? Whenever you get the urge to do something nice, follow through with it. God's light will shine through, in all the good things that you do, no matter how big or small.

Ephesians 5:8 "For you were once darkness, but now you are light in the Lord."

May 25

Show Goodness in All Things

Don't just commit part of the way to a life of righteousness. Maybe you are doing your part by getting good grades or working hard at your job, which is great. What about your behavior, though? Are you telling lies to get what you want, or cheating to get good grades? What about responsibility and respect? Do you show these to others to reflect goodness in all things? Think about the whole picture, the commitment you made to Jesus. Start living better in all areas of your life.

Ephesians 5:9 "(for the fruit of the light consists in all goodness, righteousness and truth.)"

May 26

Pleasing to Him

Living for God is something I think about a lot. Have I always thought that way? No. It has taken many years to get to this point. I have always believed in God and known of Jesus' sacrifice though. Only in later years did I truly figure out what it all meant to me and more importantly, how I might please Him. I repented and am forgiven for my sins; was baptized and believe each day I am changed. I love learning more and more about what is pleasing to God. I love knowing that I can put all my trust in Him, in all things big and small.

Ephesians 5:10 "...and find out what pleases the Lord."

May 27

He Set the Example

When Jesus was on this earth, He set the example of how God wants us to treat others. Jesus was admired by some and treated unimaginable by others, yet He treated everyone the same. Even when He knew He would be betrayed by one of His own, He did not sin against him. This is the example we should follow. We should love and be kind to each other, treating everyone the same, no matter how we are treated.

John 13:15 "I have set you an example that you should do as I have done for you."

May 28

We Are All Equal

It takes all of our body working together to complete many functions. This is also true for the jobs we are asked to do. No one job is more important than another. We cannot run a school, without both the teachers and the cafeteria workers. What about mail carriers and mail sorters? Where would one be without the other? More importantly, where would we all be without each other? Do your job the best you can, knowing it is exactly where God wants you, in His perfect plan.

John 13:16 "I tell you the truth, no servant is greater than his master, nor is a messenger greater than the one who sent him."

May 29

Imagine God's Blessing on You

Think about how good you feel when you obey your teachers, your boss or your parents. Now think about how you feel when they say nice things to you or about you because of the good job you are doing. Now, imagine God saying those things! He's noticing you and only you and how proud He is of you. Think of how truly blessed you will be when you live your life by His word. Think of how proud He will be when you obey Him.

John 13:17 "Now that you know these things, you will be blessed if you do them."

May 30

How Faithful Are You?

How faithful would you say you are? Do you trust God so much that you never worry? Do you worry all the time about what you cannot see? As I grow in my knowledge of Christ, my faith increases and I feel more at peace with my decisions. God wants us to trust Him and have faith in the unknown. When we show others, that we believe in Him, our faith will reflect outwardly to them.

Hebrews 11:1 "Now faith is being sure of what we hope for and certain of what we do not see."

May 31

Let Jesus In

It takes more than just being good, to please God and really get His attention in your life. Jesus made the ultimate sacrifice for all of us. We are offered so much more in life, when we accept Him as our Savior. If you want to get to know God, our Father, you must accept Jesus in your life first.

John 14:6 "...I am the way and the truth and the life. No one comes to the Father except through me."

June 1

Put Your Trust in the Lord, Not Man

Have you ever made plans with someone and at the last minute they cancelled? Have you ever depended on someone to be there for you and they forgot? One time I forgot to pass on an important message for someone. I apologized, but still felt very bad about it. They were hurt and I couldn't do anything to fix it. None of us are perfect. This is just another reminder, why we should put our trust in the Lord, not man.

Psalm 118:8 "It is better to take refuge in the Lord than to trust in man."

June 2

Seek Him for Peace

There have been times in my life, when I've worried about others. I have prayed very intently in many situations. I remember feeling so close to God during those times, and also so calm and at peace afterward. A peace and joy, that only our Father in heaven, could have given me. Let God help you in every situation. Seek Him, for the peace you need right now.

Psalm 94:19 "When anxiety was great within me, your consolation brought joy to my soul."

June 3

Your Hard Work Will Pay Off

One day your hard work will pay off. I know that it's hard to imagine sometimes because you have grown tired or you are ready for a change. God knows what is best for you and He knows all that you do. When you are tired, it is okay to rest. You deserve at least that much. Your hard work will pay off. Your reward will come when He comes...

Matthew 16:27 "...and then He will reward each person according to what he has done."

June 4

Find Ways to Get Involved

There are many ways you can get involved in order to help others. Think about what God has given you, how He has led you to where you are right now. What talents has He entrusted you with? What sorrows have led you to a testimonial, that you could share with someone else? If you feel that "nudge" to get involved, it's not a coincidence. Find ways to get involved and watch how God will show the way to those who will follow.

Psalm 32:8 "I will instruct you and teach you in the way you should go."

June 5

How Will You Answer These Questions?

Are you a sinner? Are you willing to turn from your sins? Do you believe Jesus Christ died for you and your sins and then rose again? Think about it...what a simple thing God has asked you to do when you are ready to answer these questions. You can pray to Him right now, with your answers and be on your way to receiving Jesus Christ in your life. Jesus made the ultimate sacrifice for us...for you! He made it simple for us to have a better life. He paid the price for our sins! Are you ready to receive His gift?

Romans 10:13 "Everyone who calls on the name of the Lord will be saved."

June 6

Save Yourself

In this world there are good things that happen daily. There are also many things that happen that aren't so good. It's hard for me to watch the news due to some of the ways people are treated. I was watching the news once and was saddened by a story of a young woman. As I was thinking about it more, I couldn't help but think about how it might have been her purpose. After all, in the long run, her sacrifice helped many others. This is a wonderful reminder that Jesus also made a sacrifice for us. If you haven't been saved, I pray you come to know Jesus as your Savior. It might determine how your challenges turn out too.

Acts 2:40 "...save your selves from this corrupt generation."

June 7

Choices Are Everywhere

We have to make decisions daily. Choices are everywhere! Some of the choices we make are simple; such as deciding what to wear or what kind of snack to have. There are also harder questions; like which college we should attend or what job to take. During your life, you might be faced with decisions that question who you are. If this happens, make sure you're making wise choices. Make decisions that help you feel good about who you are and decisions that let others know you are following God.

Luke 22:40 "...Pray that you will not fall into temptation."

June 8

Accept His Will

God wants us to pray. He wants us to ask Him for what we need. God likes when we come to Him, not only in our time of need, but also when we are thankful for what He has given us. At times in your life, you might not know how to pray and may not even know what to pray for. You'll just know you need God's guidance. Pray for His help and pray for the peace you need, to accept whatever His will may be.

Luke 22:42 "Father, if you are willing…yet not my will, but yours be done."

June 9 (Part 1)

A Fresh Coat of Paint

As I was painting once, I was glad to see all the marks on the wall disappear. It's so refreshing to walk into the room now and see the fresh new coat of paint vs. the old marked up walls. Jesus has offered that fresh new start to us too. By accepting Him as your Savior, all your sins can disappear, just like those marks on the wall. Let Jesus know you are ready to erase your old marks. He's ready to give you a fresh new start.

1 John 3:5 "But you know that He appeared so that He might take away our sins. And in Him is no sin."

June 10 (Part 2)

Fresher, Brighter, Newer

The fresh paint has covered the walls that were marked on, over the years, by furniture, kids and much more. I still find myself walking into a room, looking for some of those marks, although they have been cleared away. I believe we treat our sins the same way. Even though I know I am forgiven for my sins, sometimes I can't help but think about them. It's important to remember, that those walls are not the same, just like we are no longer the same. The walls are fresher, brighter and newer and guess what, so are you! Jesus took our sins away, just like that paint took those old marks away.

James 5:15 "...If he has sinned, he will be forgiven."

June 11

Come Quickly, To Help Me

God never changes, He is always the same. Even when you don't feel like He's there, He is. Maybe you have felt that God has come to your side late, at times. You thought He should have done something quicker or done it differently. Even though God knows your concerns, He still wants you to ask Him for what you need. Ask Him to stay near to you and ask Him to come quickly. It's what He wants from you.

Psalm 71:12 "Be not far from me O God; come quickly, O my God, to help me."

June 12

Be Responsible with Your Time

I could come home, grab a pen and paper and sit and write all night long, sometimes. Some days that sounds like a great idea! Other days, I would feel so guilty that I wouldn't even be able to enjoy that time. I think we should have a good healthy balance in our life, to enjoy some down time, some alone time and some family time. We should also have a good balance of something we like to do; maybe something you are passionate about. I believe as long as you are enjoying your time and putting God first, you can have a healthy, happy balance, that others will want to be a part of too.

John 6:27 "Do not work for food that spoils, but for food that endures to eternal life…"

June 13

Be Responsible with Your Words

The amount of words we speak each day is remarkable. It's easy sometimes to get carried away and talk forever about a subject we are interested in or care deeply about. Remember though, you should always be responsible with your words. Don't say something you'll regret because you can't take it back. You may say you're sorry, but the words you spoke are still out there. Be responsible with your words!

1 Peter 3:10 "Whoever would love life and see good days must keep their tongue from evil and their lips from deceitful speech."

June 14

Take Refuge in Him

I love knowing that no matter what I have going on in my life, I can take comfort in knowing that God is always there. We need to make sure we pray to Him, asking for what we need. Whether it is security, safety, peace or comfort, take refuge in Him, not just for this moment, but in every moment.

Psalm 16:1 "Keep me safe, O God, for in you I take refuge."

June 15

So Much Better

Many times, while writing these devotions, I prayed for those of you who would be reading them. I prayed then and still pray today, that you will be inspired to follow the Lord, have a relationship with Jesus and that you will want to tell others about this good news. I want this for you because I know what it feels like to have a relationship with Jesus. I also remember very well, my life without Him! I pray you come to know Him and want to follow Him, so that your life can be changed too. With Jesus in your life, it can be so much better!

Psalm 15:2 "...You are my Lord; apart from you I have no good thing."

June 16

The Power to Change

I am so amazed at the fact that Jesus would endure so much for us! Thinking about what He went through for you and for me, so that our sins can be forgiven, makes me so thankful to say the least. I'm forgiven of my sins…accepted into a relationship with Him…and have been given the gift of the Holy Spirit. How wonderful; knowing that I have the opportunity to change and grow, gives me all the hope that I need. It is now up to me, what I do with it. What are you doing with it?

Acts 1:8 "But you will receive power when the Holy Spirit comes on you…"

June 17

Thank God for Who You Are

Can you imagine what life would be like if we were all the same? How boring life would be if we all did the same thing every day, looked the same or had the same strengths and weaknesses? God made no mistake when He made you and He loves you just the way you are. By allowing us to be different, God also gave us the ability to see things differently. Try asking the Lord to help you recognize your weaknesses and your strengths. While you're at it, thank Him for allowing you to be different.

Genesis 1:27 "So God created man in His own image...male and female He created them."

Isaiah 64:8 "Yet you, Lord, are our Father. We are the clay, you are the potter; we are all the work of your hand."

June 18

"People Who Believe Love is Good, Meet Good People"

Quoted by Anna Ray, February 2010

The above statement is so true, love is good! It feels so good to have love in your heart, to feel love and to be in love. When we feel love, we feel better about ourselves and others. Remember, God is love, so even when you don't feel like you are loved, you are. Since God is always with you, love is always with you. If you ever feel like you are without love, ask Him to be with you, to comfort you and to help you feel loved. When He fulfills this need for love, in us, this is also true…people who believe God is love, will meet God.

1 John 4:8 "Whoever does not love does not know God, because God is love."

June 19

Every Chance You Get

Every chance you get, you should take time to learn more about God. Whether it is by reading the Bible, attending Sunday school or small group, or going to Church, you should be sure to make the most of this time. In addition to doing these things, see what else your Church offers. What kind of activities do they have for your age group? Better yet, how can you get involved, where can you help? It takes a lot of people for a Church to run. It takes even more, to spread God's news. The more you know, the more you will want to share this news with others, every chance you get.

Micah 4:2 "...He will teach us His ways, so that we may walk in His paths."

June 20

Be Gentle and Kind to Others

No matter how you feel towards someone, you should never wish something bad would happen to them. You should never be glad when they are going through bad times. Life is rough sometimes, for all of us. Would you want someone laughing at your misfortune? Be gentle and kind to others and pray for them, during their time of need. I know I'm not perfect, but I do know that I love having a relationship with Jesus. Maybe your prayer is just what someone else needs right now, for them to start their relationship with Him too.

Obadiah 1:12 "You should not look down on your brother in the day of his misfortune."

June 21

The Peace You Are Longing For

I have often wondered why my life has taken the course it has taken. Have you ever wondered why hurtful things have happened or are happening to you? Do you wonder "why me?" Good question! Why me? Why you? Why would God want me to be His friend? Why does God do all the good that He does? Why would He give up so much for me? Why is He choosing me? The answer is easy. It's because He loves us! He wants us to love Him too. Turn to Him this time, turn to Him every time. Even if you don't get all the answers you are looking for, you could get the peace you are longing for. The peace to accept Jesus in your life, so you can accept who you are and who God made you to be.

Psalm 40:1 "I waited patiently for the Lord; He turned to me and heard my cry."

June 22

Life is Too Short

There are many sayings about life being short. "Life is too short." "Time flies when you're having fun." "Enjoy every moment, it goes by fast." "Where did the time go?" These sayings are all so true, but the Bible sums it up the best.

Psalm 39:5 "Each man's life is but a breath."

Live your life to the fullest! Remember to live a life that you'll be proud of. How will you be remembered? Will people say you were kind and giving? Did you help someone along the way? Better yet, did you help anyone get saved? Our life on earth is short; don't miss your chance to spread God's news. Take every opportunity to be a reflection of God, letting others know about eternity. Remind them of how it will far outweigh our life here, which is, "but a breath."

June 23

Jesus Is by My Side

Many things in my life seem so different with Jesus by my side. Before I was saved, I would worry about little things. I was negative about the smallest of things. Now, I may not always make the right choices right away or even at all, but with Jesus in my life, I can see the brighter side to so many situations. I know I can pray in any situation and God is listening. I am so thankful for every opportunity, great and small, now that Jesus is by my side.

Psalm 40:3 "He put a new song in my mouth, a hymn of praise to our God..."

June 24

He Doesn't Want to Lose You

You should never be hard on someone or judge them for doing wrong, as if you have never done wrong. Unfortunately, there is sin on this earth and no one is exempt from it. We have all sinned and will probably continue to sin in our lives. The good news is, there is a way we can start recognizing our sin and we can each work toward being better. God loves us no matter what; He doesn't want to lose us.

Romans 3:23 "for all have sinned and fall short of the glory of God."

Romans 6:23 "For the wages of sin is death, but the gift of God is eternal life in Christ Jesus our Lord."

June 25

He Cares

Someone once said to me "Who cares!" It really made me stop and think. She was having a hard time and was having trouble seeing that anyone cared. She was hurting and when she said it, I knew she was crying out for someone to care. If you are ever in that situation and hear that cry for help or if you are the one crying for help, stop and pray. Pray to God for His peace, knowing that He cares for you.

John 14:1 "Do not let your hearts be troubled. Trust in God."

June 26

Let God Open Your Eyes

There were times in my life, when people tried preaching to me and I did not want to listen to them. I wasn't seeing things clearly and didn't understand what they were trying to tell me. Having a relationship with Jesus has changed that. It has opened my eyes to so many things. I have found the truth I needed and because of this, I am living a life that I am at peace with. Let God open your eyes to a new life...a new you.

John 9:25 "...I was blind but now I see."

June 27

Money Isn't Everything

This saying is so true, "money isn't everything!" Sure, money can buy you things, but will it make you happy? Remember to focus on what's important in life. Yes, we need money to pay for a lot of our needs and other items that we want. However, always be sure to have a good balance in all that you do. Don't work so hard to have money, that you miss out on important opportunities, especially making memories with your family and friends.

Proverbs 23:4 "Do not wear yourself out to get rich; have the wisdom to show restraint."

June 28

Better Times Will Find You

Have you ever noticed how bad luck sometimes finds those that are already down? I'm not saying bad things don't happen to everyone, I'm just saying that sometimes it's worse depending on how you are looking at life. You can grumble or you can glorify. You can look at the negative or you can look at the positive. I believe when you pursue happiness and a better life, better times will find you. Ask God to help you live a more righteous life. Ask Him to help you look for the positive in things, so you can find better times.

Proverbs 21:21 "Whoever pursues righteousness and love finds life, prosperity and honor."

June 29

How Clean Is It?

Are you living a life that you can be proud of? Are you making good choices? As my kids were growing up, I often asked them "Is your room clean?" When they answered "yes," I would ask them "Will I think it is clean?" So, when I ask you "Are you living a clean life," before you answer, let me ask you this... "Will God think it is?"

Proverbs 21:2 "All a man's ways seem right to him, but the Lord weighs the heart."

June 30 (Part 1)

Use Your Knowledge Wisely

There are many ways to increase your knowledge of Christ. What are you doing with that knowledge, though? Are you obeying it? Are you putting it to good use? Are you sharing what you've learned with others? We will gain so much knowledge in our lives. However, if we are not practicing these good ways, we are not very wise. Don't just gain this information, obey it and share it with others. Use your knowledge wisely!

Daniel 12:3 "Those who are wise will shine like the brightness of the heavens…"

July 1 (Part 2)

Reflect God's Goodness

Growing in God's word is the best way to increase your knowledge of Christ. Reading the bible daily will help you put God's word to use. By sharing what you've learned, you can help lead others to Christ. Whether you are teaching it or sharing it, by living a Christlike life, you can forever reflect God's goodness.

Daniel 12:3 "...and those who lead many to righteousness (will shine) like the stars forever and ever."

July 2 (Part 1)

I Know God Is Speaking to Me

As I put these devotions together, to share with all of you, I know God is also speaking to me, through these words. I like the reminders He gives me each day. Is it always easy for me? No. Do I always make the best choices? No. I do try my best, though. I love knowing that He created me, He loves me and He always watches over me.

Job 10:12 "You gave me life and showed me kindness, and in your providence watched over my spirit."

July 3 (Part 2)

He Is Watching Over Us

When you pray, believe that what you are asking for, has already been done for you. Trusting and believing are the biggest steps to faith, that you will ever have. When I pray, I often thank God in advance for watching over us. By putting my faith first, I can be at peace knowing that He will answer my prayers. They may not always be the answers I was expecting, but I love knowing that I'm not alone and that God is watching over me. Put your trust in Him and remember that He knows what is best for you. Believe, that no matter how He answers your prayers, it is the way He intended it to be.

Matthew 8:13 "Go! It will be done just as you believed it would."

July 4

I Will Trust in Him

I'll admit, I have been afraid of many things in my life. My biggest fear is heights, but my fear of speaking in front of people, is at the top of my list too. When I have blindly gone into a speech without praying, I have been so nervous. Having a relationship with Jesus, I know I can pray and He will be with me. I know I can ask for His guidance and He will give me the words to speak. He helps me remain calm, when I put my trust in Him. Whenever you are afraid, trust Him to help you through it.

Psalm 56:3 "When I am afraid, I will trust in you."

July 5

A Renewed Spirit

I've said things before and then wished I hadn't said them. Has that ever happened to you? Have you ever had a time in your life, when no matter what you did, you couldn't get your thoughts turned to more positive thinking? Maybe you were just having a bad day and everything seemed kind of dull or maybe you just felt negative about everything. If or when this happens, ask God to help you see things in a different light. Ask Him to help you rest in His thoughts.

Psalm 51:10 "Create in me a pure heart, O God, and renew a steadfast spirit within me."

July 6

Imagine the Glory

Jesus has done so much for us! He has offered us a free gift and all we have to do is believe. Jesus died for our sins! When we believe this, we can have a wonderful relationship with Him, here on earth. Now, imagine that glory, when we are with Him in Heaven...forever.

John 11:40 "Then Jesus said, 'Did I not tell you that if you believed, you would see the glory of God?'"

July 7

Stormy Weather

Stormy weather sometimes scares me. The worst part is making the decision to get somewhere safe, especially in the middle of the night, when everyone is sleeping. During those times I have probably prayed harder than any other times in my life. I do this because I need God's guidance, His peace and His comfort. I cannot get through the storms on my own. I need Him to lead me. By putting my trust in Him, I can be a better leader for those around me, so they may also find their peace and comfort in Him.

Matthew 8:27 "The men were amazed and asked, 'What kind of man is this? Even the winds and the waves obey Him?'"

July 8

Accept His Grace in Our Differences

When we compare ourselves to others, we are forgetting several things. We have forgotten that we are supposed to be different. We each have different abilities that we are able to bring forward. What if we were all teaching the same lesson or writing down the same thoughts? How would we ever learn anything new? How would we ever be inspired to create something unique? I think it's important that we accept who we are and not compare ourselves to anyone else. We should be thankful for the gifts He has given us and always remember that God made us just the way He wants us.

Romans 12:6-8 "We have different gifts, according to the grace given to each of us. If your gift is prophesying, then prophesy in accordance with your faith; if it is serving, then serve; if it is teaching, then teach; if it is to encourage, then give encouragement; if it is giving, then give generously; if it is to lead, do it diligently; if it is to show mercy, do it cheerfully."

July 9

We Need to Pray

We were rushing around one morning, getting everything ready for vacation. As soon as we got on the interstate, I remembered we needed to pray! In our busyness, I had forgotten to pray for our safe travels, forgotten to ask God to watch over us. What helped me remember? As we were getting on the interstate, a truck pulled over in front of us and I mean right in front of us! I knew we could take that moment and start our vacation in a panic or we could relax and pray. Traffic makes me nervous, fast speeds do too. However, when I turn it over to God and have faith in His plan, It is definitely a much more relaxing trip.

Jeremiah 17:7 "But blessed is the man who trusts in the Lord, whose confidence is in Him."

July 10 (Part 1)

He Speaks to Me through Others

While reading a book, I couldn't help but think about how God was speaking to me, through that book. Many times, and in many ways, I have also felt God speak to me through others. Whether it is in their story or in their actions, I have felt as though He wanted me to hear Him, through them. I pray that God will continue to speak to us, but I pray most of all, that we will listen when He does.

Romans 10:20 "...I was found by those who did not seek me."

July 11 (Part 2)

He Whispers

It's important to have quiet time to reflect on your life and what God has done for you. I have often heard more from God, in times when I wasn't even expecting it. When I am pulling weeds or doing laundry or the dishes, I feel as if He whispers to me. His words become my thoughts, as if we are one. It is during those times, that I am so thankful for the Holy Spirit and for the opportunity to hear Him.

Ephesians 2:18 "For through Him we both have access to the Father by one Spirit."

July 12 (Part 1)

Helping Others Walk by Faith

While we were at a waterpark once, we came across a woman who appeared very scared, when she heard a storm was coming. The storm had not officially started yet, but we were walking to shelter because the wind was picking up and dark clouds were rolling in. All of a sudden, the woman started yelling at everyone and panicking. Unfortunately, it made others around us, especially the younger children, panic too. It turned out to be a good lesson in faith for our family. We were able to pray for the woman and anyone else that needed His guidance during the storm that day. By praying for our comfort and safety, we were able to show our kids, how at peace we could remain.

Romans 12:13 "Share with God's people who are in need. Practice hospitality."

July 13 (Part 2)

Walking by Faith

I've been in some unsafe places during some pretty severe storms. I've been in a treehouse cabin during Church camp. I've been in a boat in the middle of a lake trying to get to safe ground. I've even been huddled together with many others under a locker island at a water park. During those moments, every silent thought I had, I turned to God to help me stay calm. Walking by faith in those times helped me know, that whatever His plan was for me, I would be okay. When you reflect that peace, it keeps the atmosphere around you calm as well.

Romans 1:12 (NCV) "I want us to help each other with the faith we have. Your faith will help me, and my faith will help you."

July 14

What Are You Passionate About?

Think about your favorite thing to do...your passion. What is it that you do that makes you feel good whenever you are doing it? Now, think about how you can use that passion to let others know about Jesus. Ask God to help you use your passion to share His good news. Don't ever underestimate the possibilities!

John 7:18 "He who speaks on his own does so to gain honor for himself, but he who works for the honor of the one who sent him is a man of truth; there is nothing false about him."

July 15

You Are Right Where He Wants You

A series of events took place that could have made a real impact on how we looked at our vacation. Seems like one thing would happen, only for us to be looking at another unfortunate situation. Was our vacation ruined because of it? No. Each time we focused on God and the good things in the situation. We believed through it all, that we were right where He intended. We knew handling it with a "meant to be" attitude was wiser than "why me" or "why now?" Remember, whatever you go through, you are right where He wants you. Turn to Him when you need Him the most.

Ephesians 1:11 "In Him we were also chosen, having been predestined according to the plan of Him who works out everything in conformity with the purpose of His will."

July 16

Go to God for Comfort

Maybe you are hurting because you lost a loved one. Maybe you lost your job or you are just unhappy with what you are doing. It's okay to admit you are hurting. No matter what it is, you can always go to God for comfort. Ask for what you need, and watch Him work in your life. Let others know you are hurting, so they can pray for you too. When we come to God in prayer and let Him know we can't handle it on our own, that is when the true healing begins.

2 Corinthians 1:5 "For just as the sufferings of Christ flow over into our lives, so also through Christ our comfort overflows."

July 17

Seeing His Great Power

It's so amazing seeing the great power that God has. One minute it's storming and raining very hard and the next minute it is calm and the birds are chirping. It's easy to see the beauty in things once the storm has passed. Remember to look for the beauty within the storm too. Think about how that rain will help the flowers grow. The wind helps dry up the puddles on the surface. It's so amazing seeing it all come together and the beauty within. It's so amazing seeing the great power that God has.

Ephesians 1:19 "and His incomparably great power for us who believe. That power is like the working of His mighty strength."

July 18

Perfect in His Eyes

The greatest thing, about what Jesus did for us, is that He did it for ALL of us. In a world where we're judged by our looks, our jobs and our possessions, it is wonderful knowing that God doesn't look at us that way. God loves us...we are perfect in His eyes! He wants us ALL to accept His gift.

Luke 2:10 "But the angel said to them, 'Do not be afraid. I bring you good news of great joy that will be for all the people.'"

July 19 (Part 1)

Keep A Clear Heart

I knew the truth about something once, but when I asked the person involved, I was given a different answer. I wasn't mad at that person though. I wasn't even upset. You know what I did? I prayed for them. I prayed they could see themselves in the situation and look to God for a clear heart. I also took the opportunity to teach my own kids about making sure they always tell the truth. If you are ever tempted to lie about something, pray and ask God to show you how to keep a clear heart.

Proverbs 16:13 "Kings take pleasure in honest lips; they value a man who speaks the truth."

July 20 (Part 2)

They Need Our Prayers

My kids saw an example of someone lying once and they had some questions about it. While discussing and praying about the situation, it became clear to me, that it would not do any good to get upset with that person. It also became clear to me, that when people lie, it is because they need our prayers. Lying usually comes into the picture because someone is guilty about what they did or they know they did something wrong. Stay true to who you are! Stay truthful in all you do and most of all, BE truthful. When someone doesn't show these qualities to you, be kind and patient with them even more.

Proverbs 19:11 "A man's wisdom gives him patience; it is to his glory to overlook an offense."

July 21

Go with the Flow

Have you ever been in the ocean trying to swim against the waves? Maybe you've been in a wave pool at a water park and tried to swim against the waves there. It's hard isn't it? It doesn't feel natural. Life is that way too sometimes. We go through situations that we think we need to work against, but it doesn't feel quite right. Obstacles are in our way and it feels like we're fighting to get through them. Rather than do that, we need to ask God for the power to be still and go with the flow. Let Him lead you where He wants you. Don't fight the waves!

Proverbs 19:21 "Many are the plans in a man's heart, but it is the Lord's purpose that prevails."

July 22

Do Whatever You Can to Help Others

Watching a film about a country struggling to get clean water really made me stop and think. We take things for granted! We know that we can walk in the kitchen, turn on the faucet and water will come out. Even if it doesn't, we can call a plumber to get it fixed and soon water will come out again. We are so fortunate to live in a country where we have so much. Do whatever you can to help those around you, who aren't as fortunate.

'Lord, let us see the good in all that we have. Help us to recognize there is need in this world. Give us the courage to do whatever we can to help others. In Jesus' name, Amen!'

Matthew 5:42 "Give to the one who asks you, and do not turn away from the one who wants to borrow from you."

July 23

What Would Jesus Do?

When I think of myself all the time, I am not just hurting others I am also hurting myself. Some examples of this are, only picking up after myself or always making plans to make sure I get what I want. How would that make others around me feel? What about cleaning up after each other or making sure everyone is included? When I only think of myself, people get hurt and in the long run, I end up feeling bad about it. Instead of thinking of myself first, in every situation, I should always ask the question, "What would Jesus do?"

Philippians 2:4 "not looking to your own interest but each of you to the interests of the others."

1 Peter 1:15 "But just as He who called you is holy, so be holy in all you do; for it is written: 'Be holy because I am holy.'"

July 24

Until I Really Knew Him

I've known and believed in God for as long as I can remember. However, it wasn't until I really knew Him and began a relationship with Jesus, that I was able to begin a life of worrying less and focusing more. Focusing my time and energy on pleasing Him, rather than myself or others. It has taught me more than I could ever imagine! Let God lead you, so you can really get to know Him too.

Psalm 71:17 "Since my youth, O God, you have taught me, and to this day I declare your marvelous deeds."

July 25

God Chose You

Isn't it comforting knowing that you have God on your side? God is not only there for you; He wants to be there for you. Perhaps you remember being called to Him.   Maybe you knew you needed something more in your life. Maybe you knew you wanted to be a better person or you wanted to live a better life. Whatever it was, you felt His love and you felt Him calling you. Aren't you glad He chose you?

1 Peter 2:9 "But you are a chosen people, a royal priesthood, a holy nation, a people belonging to God, that you may declare the praises of Him who called you out of darkness into His wonderful light."

July 26

I Promise To

I promise to...what? What kind of promises do you make? Do you always keep your promises? How do you feel when others break their promises to you? The biggest question of all, how would you feel if God broke His promises to you? Thankfully, we don't have to worry about that. God's promises are written for us to learn, to live by and to share with others. God reminds us often that when we keep our promises and stay true to Him, we are promised more than we can ever imagine.

Deuteronomy 6:3 "...just as the Lord, the God of your fathers, promised you."

July 27 (Part 1)

Treat Each Other With Kindness

I remember years ago hearing a story at a seminar that made me stop and think. Years later, I reheard a version of that same story at church. Basically, when we are treated badly, we tend to turn around and treat others badly too. In the above-mentioned stories, the bad reaction from the people involved, trickled down all the way to their cat. I often wonder sometimes when I'm treated badly, what is really going on in that person's life? Did I deserve to be talked to that way? Did they really mean it the way it sounded? No matter how you are spoken to, remember to always treat others the way you want to be treated. No one wants to be treated badly, not even your cat.

Psalm 27:12 "Do not turn me over to the desire of my foes..."

July 28 (Part 2)

Pay It Back/Pay It Forward

Our local Christian radio station promotes a "Pay It Back" series. It's a way for listeners to do something kind for someone...just because. Wouldn't it be great if we all put that into motion every day? I've heard of people paying for the next person's food at the drive-thru and have done that a time or two myself. One person mentioned they even picked someone up and gave them a ride because they were waiting for a bus in the rain. What we do for each other doesn't have to be extreme, just kind. It doesn't take much to give a smile or a thank you or to even open a door for someone. Think about how much you'll enjoy passing on good deeds to others. Who knows, maybe someone will even pay you back.

Proverbs 22:9 "A generous man will himself be blessed, for he shares his food with the poor."

July 29

He Knows Your Heart

Do you ever really get to know someone? How do you explain who they are? Do you mention their hair color or whether or not they wear glasses? Is that really who they are? I could describe someone to you, but you wouldn't know much about them until you really got to know them. Who someone is, isn't what's on the outside, it comes from within. Even when you think you know everything about that person, you probably don't. No one knows your heart except you and your creator. There are no secrets with God. He knows your heart and loves every inch of who you are.

Proverbs 27:19 "As water reflects a face, so a man's heart reflects the man."

July 30 (Part 1)

Godly Advice

We were once asked in Sunday school where we go for advice. Through the years, I have gone to many different people for advice. Sometimes I have heard just what I wanted to hear and other times it's not quite been what I wanted or expected to hear. No matter what, the best advice has been the advice that has led me to God. Sometimes the advice has come from a family member or a close friend. Other times, it has been given to me directly, a gentle whisper...a slight nudge. Whenever I am reminded to focus on God, I know I have been given the best advice of all.

Romans 11:36 "For from Him and through Him and to Him all things. To Him be the glory forever! Amen."

July 31 (Part 2)

He Listens to Me

Many times, I've gone to others to be heard. I've just needed someone to listen to me. Over the years, as I have developed a relationship with Jesus, I've found someone to do just that. God listens to me, without interrupting and without judging. He knows what I'm thinking; I don't even have to say anything. Through prayer, I have asked for guidance on many occasions. Through silence, He listens and answers me. I pray that we could all be good listeners to Him in return.

Revelation 2:7 "He who has an ear, let him hear what the Spirit says to the churches."

August 1

In the Nick of Time

I heard on the news one morning; a lady was saved "in the nick of time." She was swept away in a flood and nearly drowned. She was close to going over a cliff but was rescued by a man who swam out to help her. Does this resemble your story of when you were saved? Are you still trying to decide if you are ready to be saved? Do you feel like you are drowning, but unable to get help? Don't wait until the "nick of time" or until it is too late. God wants to rescue you. Reach out for Him; let Him know how close you are to drowning. Let Him know you are ready to be saved.

Luke 12:40 "You also must be ready, because the Son of Man will come at an hour when you do not expect Him."

August 2 (Part 1)

My BFF

At different times in my life I have had different "best friends." Growing up, my best friend lived in my neighborhood and we were always running back and forth between our houses. Later, going through school I had a different best friend and enjoyed spending a lot of time with her. As I grew older and met my husband, of course, he became and still is my best friend. I also consider my kids and many of my family members my best friends. Do all my friends and family know everything about me? No. Can they be with me everywhere I go? No, but they are still my friends. Imagine having a friend that knows you better than you know yourself. God created you to be exactly who you are and He will love you your whole life and beyond. He knows everything about you and loves you just the same. A best friend forever!

"Isaiah 26:4 "Trust in the Lord forever, for the Lord, the Lord, is the Rock eternal."

August 3 (Part 2)

Come as You Are

When I worked a job where I had the summers off, most days I didn't bother putting on make-up and I rarely did my hair. I figured no one really cared and I would just put my hair back, since it was a lot easier anyway. My husband tells me often that I don't need make-up and fancy hair dos anyway. When people love each other it's easy to see them for who they really are and accept them no matter what. We know what they are like on the inside and that's how God wants it to be. That is how He sees us. He accepts us no matter what! He loves us for who we are and calls us to Him. He doesn't care if our hair is done or if we have make-up on or not. It's as if He is telling us to just "come as you are."

Proverbs 20:27 "The lamp of the Lord searches the spirit of a man, it searches out his inmost being."

August 4

Use Your Money Wisely

I will never forget an answer to prayer during a time in our life when we were struggling with money. Many times, I had asked God for more money but that wasn't what I needed and it wasn't what He wanted for me either. One night I was praying and I asked God to help us use the money we had more wisely. I couldn't believe at church the very next day, we were told about a financial class they were going to be offering. I knew right away that it was an answer from God...not more money, but a way to use the money we had more wisely.

Psalm 34:4 "I sought the Lord, and He answered me; He delivered me from all my fears."

August 5

Do Not Envy

None of us have the same taste. We all have different decorating ideas and different styles and that's okay. Actually, its's better than okay, it is the way it's supposed to be. Think about how boring it would be if everyone dressed the same or we all lived in houses that looked the same or were decorated the same. With that in mind, make sure you don't love what someone else has more than what you have. Nothing is wrong with admiring it, but you shouldn't envy so much that you dread your own belongings.

Proverbs 14:30 "A heart at peace gives life to the body, but envy rots the bones."

August 6

Let Me Have It

Through the years, my kids fought over this or that toy or this or that book. Sometimes they even fought over who should have the TV remote. As a parent I often said to them "let me have it." I wanted them to realize that if they couldn't figure it out or talk nice to each other, they needed to turn it over. God knows we can't always figure it out on our own. He wants us to get along with everyone in every situation. Remember every day, God wants you to turn your struggles over to Him. Can you hear Him? He's saying "let me have it."

1 Peter 5:7 "Cast all your anxiety on Him because He cares for you."

Lamentations 3:25 "The Lord is good to those whose hope is in Him, to the one who seeks Him."

August 7

Great Is Your Faithfulness

With the Lord you cannot fail! You may think you have failed because you didn't get the job you wanted or your plans didn't go the way you wanted. It may not have worked out as you pictured it, but perhaps He's painting a new picture. A picture just for you, a picture that only He knows what it will look like. Trust in Him and have faith in the outcome. I'm sure the picture will be worth the wait.

Lamentations 3:22-23 "Because of the Lord's great love we are not consumed, for His compassions never fail. They are new every morning; great is your faithfulness."

August 8

God Will Lead You

I'll never forget the day we found out that a co-worker's dad had passed away. We had only found out that he was sick, just a short time before. He had options and was a man of faith, so he felt the choice was clear. He put it in God's hands! Truly that is the only way it should be. Don't make choices without consulting Him first. Never make choices, especially hard choices, by yourself. God will lead you if you let Him.

Mark 6:50 "Take courage! It is I. Don't be afraid."

August 9

A Child of God

I am so thankful for my relationship with Jesus! I'm thankful that in the smallest of things, I can see His work and recognize Him. It's hard for me to remember a time when I didn't know Him. I always knew He was there, but I didn't always focus on Him. I'm glad to know now, that He believed in me all along. I'm thankful that I have found a relationship with Jesus. I truly believe, once a child of God...always a child of God."

Philippians 2:14 "Do everything without complaining or arguing, so that you may become blameless and pure, children of God without fault in a crooked and depraved generation, in which you shine like stars in the universe..."

August 10

God's Presence Is There

Working at a school in this day and age it's hard to believe that anyone would take prayer out of school. We need prayer in school for many reasons. During my lifetime alone, there have been many mass shootings. We are also seeing more and more kids with emotional disabilities. While I was working for a local school, one day I was looking around in the library and I saw something! In the windows, the window frames were in the shape of crosses. It was comforting to me to be reminded that God is truly there. Do I have to see a sign to know it? No. Does that mean He's not there if I don't see anything? No. It's just good to know that when we have Him in our hearts and bring Him with us, no law is bigger than our God!

Philippians 1:18 "But what does it matter? The important thing is that in every way, whether from false motives or true, Christ is preached. And because of this I rejoice!"

August 11

Help Me Know What to Say

'Lord, give me the words to speak, so I will always know just what to say. Help me to share your word with others and let them see you through me! I pray this in your son's name. Amen!'

God puts us in the path of many different types of people. Many people know God and others believe, but may not have a relationship with Him. There are still many more people we need to be telling about God and sharing the wonderful news of salvation. I don't always know what to say to everyone, every time we are together. I pray though, that my words and actions, will make a positive difference toward eternal life for them.

Ephesians 6:19 "Pray also for me, that whenever I open my mouth, words may be given me so that I will fearlessly make known the mystery of the gospel…"

August 12

My Voice Is Heard

Over the years I have prayed for close friends, family members and even people I haven't known. Sometimes my prayers have been answered right away and other times they have taken a while. Even when my prayers aren't answered the way I want, I still know my voice is heard. God is listening! Pray to Him and let your voice be heard.

Psalm 66:19 "but God has surely listened and heard my voice in prayer."

August 13 (Part 1)

Not by Luck, but For a Reason

My birthday is August 13 (8-13). Some people think of the number 13 as bad luck, but I don't! That's the day I was born. I never look at it as a bad luck/good luck thing. Knowing God put me on this earth for a reason is all the inspiration I need. I always rejoice in the fact, that He chose me to come here to help fulfill His plan, exactly when He wanted me here.

Revelation 22:7 "…Blessed is he who keeps the words of the prophecy in this book."

August 14 (Part 2)

Meant to Be

Sometimes I can't help but notice when the time turns to 8:13. I always kiddingly, point it out to my husband and kids, since those are my birthday numbers. Many times, when these numbers have come up together in some way, I've gotten that "meant to be" feeling. For example, when I was asked to teach at our VBS for the first time, I thought it was pretty neat how God worked it out. My lesson ended up being Matthew 8:10-13. He gave me just the right amount of courage to say "yes," knowing that it was meant to be. Where do you see your signs of things that are meant to be?

Deuteronomy 4:35 "You were shown these things so that you might know that the Lord is God..."

August 15

A Smile Goes a Long Way

It's hard for me to understand why some people don't smile. Life is not always easy, but why make it harder? A simple smile can go a long way, especially when someone has given you one or someone else really needs one. At times, I've thought that if they are not going to return the smile, I won't give it. As a Christian, I've realized that they need it that much more. Maybe your smile is the only one they've seen in a long time. Let your smile be a comfort to someone else. Let it be a reflection of Christ.

1 Corinthians 11:1 "Follow my example, as I follow the example of Christ."

August 16

You Deserve It...Believe It!

Often times, I've heard the phrase "You deserve it." I wonder how many of those times the person hearing it actually believes it. We are our own worst critics. We don't always believe the good things we hear about ourselves. It's usually easier to believe the bad things. You worked hard today, take a break, you deserve it! You can be forgiven for your sins...let God know you are ready...You truly do deserve it! Believe it!!

2 Timothy 2:10 "Therefore I endure everything for the sake of the elect, that they too may obtain the salvation that is in Christ Jesus, with eternal glory."

August 17

The Word of Truth

I received a card once from a good friend and co-worker. It was so nice! She talked about how she missed me and how it just wasn't the same, since we were not working together anymore. It took me by surprise when tears came to my eyes. I realized how much I missed her too! Isn't it nice to know you are needed and how much someone cares for you? God wants us to know how much He cares for us. He wants us to feel that love every day.

James 1:18 (NCV) "God decided to give us life through the word of truth so we might be the most important of all things He made."

August 18

Stay True to Him

Have you ever been in a really good mood and then come in contact with someone who wasn't very happy? It's happened to me on many occasions. It's hard to get that good feeling back sometimes. With God in my life, thankfully I feel like He often gives me that "nudge" I need to get back on track. By staying true to Him and staying true to His word, it will help you keep a better attitude. You might even help someone else find the peace they are looking for, so they can be happy too.

2 Thessalonians 3:2 "And pray that we may be delivered from wicked and evil men, for not everyone has faith."

August 19

Ask "What" Not "Why"

I know I have asked "why" during many situations.

"Why me?" "Why now?"

"Why is this happening this way?" "Why?"

Instead of asking "Why," try asking "What?" "What purpose does God want me to fulfill?" "What does God want me to learn from this?" "What direction does God want me to take?" When we ask "what" instead of "why" we're trusting Him and realizing how much He is in control. We know He has a plan for us. We just don't know what.

Romans 8:18 "I consider that our present sufferings are not worth comparing with the glory that will be revealed in us."

August 20

The Right Time to Say Something

How do you handle people that aren't easy to get along with? How do you decide what to say to them? Walking away and holding your tongue shows a lot of strength. When we stop the situation from getting worse, it shows them a better way to handle things, a better way of dealing with it. Pray to God and ask Him to give you the words to speak. Ask Him to help you know when it is the right time to say something or if it is best to walk away.

James 5:9 "Don't grumble against each other, brothers, or you will be judged."

August 21

Open 24 Hours

My son wrote in his journal at school one time, about going to his Grandma's house. He said that it was open 24 hours. When I was sharing it with my mom, she reminded me that she has a sign by the door that says "Welcome to Grandma's, Open 24 Hours." I have seen the sign many times but had forgotten about it. He was just learning to read at that time, so it was fresh on his mind. No matter where we are in our walk, let's never forget that it's the same with God because heaven never closes. Although we may forget at times, God doesn't forget about us. He stays open for us all the time...after all He is open 24 hours.

2 Peter 3:8 "But do not forget this one thing, dear friends; With the Lord a day is like a thousand years and a thousand years are like a day."

August 22

The Greatness in His Creation

It always seems that whenever it has been really hot out, our conversations always start with or at some point end up being about the weather. Wouldn't it be nice to get up and notice the good things about the weather? One of my favorite things about the weather is how after it rains really hard, we get a gentle breeze to dry up the puddles. I love how green everything looks after it has rained and the sun comes out. God has a perfect plan for all living things. We may think it's too much of one thing or not enough of another, but He knows what He's doing. In time, we will all see and appreciate His perfect plan. For now, notice a good thing about the weather each day and share it with someone else. Passing on the greatness of His creation is a wonderful plan.

Habakkuk 1:5 "Look at the nations and watch and be utterly amazed."

August 23 (Part 1)

We Can See Them Again

Losing a loved one is probably one of the hardest things we'll ever go through, during our time on earth. They're gone; they'll no longer be living here with us. We miss them more than words can say! The good news is, we can see them again. Have you confessed your sins to God? Have you let God know you believe in Him and want to one day live with Him forever in heaven? If not, pray to Him now for the courage and the guidance to help you get to that point. God wants us to be with our loved ones again. He wants us all to come home to Him.

1 Peter 1:4 "and into an inheritance that can never perish, spoil or fade-kept in heaven for you."

August 24 (Part 2)

We Will See Them Again

When a loved one passes on, we are saddened beyond belief. It's hard accepting the fact that we won't see them again during our time on earth. That's what we need to remember though. We won't see them here, but we will see them again, if we have repented and accepted Jesus in our lives. The hope we receive from that alone, can help us get through it. They've gone somewhere wonderful and we should rejoice for them. We know this, yet it's hard to accept. God will get you through it, though! Ask Him for the peace and comfort you need. Know that your loved one is no longer hurting and that one day, you wlll both be in heaven...together.

1 Peter 1:9 "for you are receiving the goal of your faith, the salvation of your souls."

August 25 (Part 1)

Do Your Best Work for Him

There might be times in your life when you may not enjoy the job you're doing or the class you are taking. Its times like these when we need to be reminded, that we shouldn't be doing anything for ourselves anyway. God wants us to show others His beautiful glory. When we are in situations such as these, we need to share God's glory with everyone we can. Continue doing your best work no matter what, not for yourself, but for Him!

Psalm 51:12 "Restore to me the joy of your salvation and grant me a willing spirit, to sustain me."

August 26 (Part 2)

His Plan for Others, Through Us

I am so thankful for a discussion I had recently with a Christian friend. She reminded me that God places us where He does for many reasons. It's always for Him. However, sometimes He's fulfilling His plan for others, through us. Maybe He's placing you where you are, so that you can tell others His good news. You might be the only one who will share it with them. You might be the only one they will listen to. Do your work for Him. In doing so, you may get the chance to tell someone where your faith and your hope come from.

Romans 15:21 "...Those who were not told about Him will see, and those who have not heard will understand."

August 27

Take the Godly Approach

I've had many bosses during my life and have worked in many different jobs. My happiest times have been when I've worked for people that have appreciated and respected their employees. Some bosses use their power or the fact that they are "in charge" to be too bossy. This approach really doesn't work. You end up with employees who complain and gossip. Whatever you are in charge of, I pray that you take the godly approach. God lets us do our work while He watches over us. He loves us and lets us learn from our own mistakes. Isn't it great doing God's work, knowing He loves and cares for us so much? Don't you want to do and be your best, when you are appreciated?

Psalm 66:7 "He rules forever by His power; His eyes watch the nations – let not the rebellious rise up against Him."

August 28

Home Sweet Home

Imagine yourself running the bases after you've hit a homerun during a ball game. Doesn't it feel good running around the bases knowing you're going to make it "home?" How about after you've been on vacation for a long time? Don't you love the feeling of being home again, in your own bed, in your own house? Now, imagine knowing that one day, if you have accepted Jesus as your Savior, you will be with Him forever in heaven. Imagine being with him in your new Home Sweet Home.

Revelation 21:1 "Then I saw a new heaven and a new earth..."

August 29 (Part 1)

God Remains with You

Certain events in my life have been so unforgettable. It's easy to remember the details about where I was when they happened and how I felt about them. I know many events have even brought me closer to God. Depending on the situation, whether I was scared or thankful, I know God was with me. Isn't it wonderful knowing, that no matter where you are, God remains with you throughout every moment?

Matthew 28:20 "...And surely I am with you always, to the very end of the age."

August 30 (Part 2)

Preparing for That Perfect Place

Hearing a song on the radio one day helped me realize something. We will go through difficult times. Many of them, we'll wish we could skip altogether. However, God has made a perfect plan. Each step must happen in order for us to get to that perfect place. Next time you go through a moment, that you wish you could skip, ask God to allow you to help prepare for that perfect place, at the perfect time.

Revelation 21:4 "...There will be no more death or mourning or crying or pain..."

August 31

One Thing Will Never Change

I've been thinking a lot about the many ways our lives can change. One day we're content in our job and the next day something changes. Maybe someone quits or someone new gets hired. Our lives are always changing. Change is hard and we don't always understand why things must change, yet they do. When you go through changes it may not feel right at first, but remember God will be with you...that will never change!

James 1:17 "Every good and perfect gift is from above, coming down from the Father of the heavenly lights, who does not change like shifting shadows."

September 1

People Come and Go in Our Lives

Some friends move in, while others move away. Loved ones pass on and we begin to pray.

We pray for comfort and peace, and for the strength to go on.

When our hearts are still hurting, how can we go on?

Keep your focus on God; He will not let you down.

Keep your focus on Him, so one day you'll wear your crown.

One day you'll know the reasons why, and that happy day you will no longer cry.

2 Timothy 4:8 "Now there is in store for me the crown of righteousness, which the Lord, the righteous Judge, will award to me on that day – and not only to me, but also to all who have longed for His appearing."

September 2

Do with It What You Will

I was reading my journal entries from one of the times I read "The Purpose Driven Life." At the end of one statement I wrote "Do with it what you will," a common phrase that I hadn't thought much about. Thinking about it now, it's easy to see those words in a different light. Lord, do with it what you will. Do with me what you will. Help us to see it's not about us, but about your will for us.

Matthew 7:21 "Not everyone who says to me, 'Lord, Lord'; will enter the kingdom of heaven, but only he who does the will of my Father who is in heaven."

September 3

God Made No Mistakes When He Made You

Maybe there's something about you that you don't like or you wish you could change. There have been things I have wanted to change during my life. However, would I still be me? Would I be the person He wants me to be? God made no mistakes when he made me; He made no mistakes when He made you. He made us in His image, and we are capable of so much if we follow His commands for us.

Deuteronomy 7:9 "Know therefore that the Lord your God is God; He is the faithful God, keeping His covenants of love to a thousand generations of those who love Him and keep His commands."

September 4

Pray Together

Our Pastor recently mentioned the fact that fewer and fewer families sit down and eat their meals together anymore. I remember when we first moved in to our house, my brother mentioned that to me too. He thought it was nice that we did that with our kids. If it's not something you do, maybe you could try it. It's a good time to focus on your family, and your faith, praying together, so you can focus on Him...together.

Psalm 78:2-3 "I will open my mouth in parables, I will utter hidden things, things from of old-what we have heard and known, what our fathers have told us."

September 5

The More I Know, the More I Want to Know

Have you ever had the feeling that you just wanted more? Maybe you've wanted another helping at dinner or another bite of dessert. Have you ever wanted to keep reading your book and just kept saying "one more chapter" over and over again? I've felt that way about a lot of things, but nothing compares to the feeling I get knowing Jesus. The more I know, the more I want to know.

Psalm 143:6 "I spread out my hands to you; my soul thirsts for you like a parched land."

September 6

How Is God Calling You to Share His Word?

I have wanted to write for as long as I can remember. I haven't always known what I wanted to write about, I just knew I wanted to write. God has led me to a place where He knows I will share His word. Writing and telling others about Him is something I feel very passionate about. I love when I have opportunities to tell others about Jesus. I feel so blessed when I am able to share what I know. How is God calling you to share His word?

Psalm 145:11 "They will tell of the glory of your kingdom and speak of your might, so that all men may know of your mighty acts and the glorious splendor of your kingdom."

September 7 (Part 1)

It's for Your Own Good

"It's for your own good!" I'm sure we've all heard these words at some point in our lives. We probably didn't want to hear them, especially when we were too young to understand the reasons behind them. Praying is that way too. We may not always realize why a prayer is not answered the way we want it to be. Perhaps, if we listen close enough, we can hear God telling us, "no, it's for your own good."

Psalm 75:2 "You say, 'I choose the appointed time; it is I who judge uprightly."

September 8 (Part 2)

Tough Love

Have you ever had to tell someone "no," for their own good? Unfortunately, when it comes to tough love, we'll all go through it sooner or later. Whether we're the ones being told "no" or the parent having to tell their child "no." We've all had to learn right from wrong at some point, hopefully sooner rather than later. God must feel the same way when we make bad choices. No one likes to see their child sin or to have to tell them "no." However, showing your child you care enough to say "no," knowing it's for their own good, is the greatest love you can give them.

Psalm 66:18 "If I had cherished sin in my heart, the Lord would not have listened."

September 9

Leave a Message

Have you ever left a message on someone's voice mail and afterward worried about how you sounded? Maybe you rambled on and on or wondered if you made sense. Then there's always the "phone voice" that you might use when you don't quite sound like yourself. Praying is sort of like leaving a message, isn't it? You are able to talk as long as you want, whenever you want, without interruption. The great thing is that God doesn't care if you sound silly or say too much. He just wants you to "leave a message."

Psalm 66:20 "Praise be to God, who has not rejected my prayer or withheld His love from me."

September 10

Let God Speak to You

When I first started writing these devotions, I remember setting goals with them. At first, I thought I would write so much each day. I also wanted to get it done by a certain time of year. The more I got involved with it, the more I realized there was no need to set goals with it. I liked them better when I allowed the words to come to me, when I allowed God to speak to me. Whatever you are doing, let God speak to you, let Him show you the way.

John 4:26 "Then Jesus declared 'I who speak to you am He.'"

September 11

Feeling God's Presence

I have attended many ceremonies for the men, women and children in our country that died during a terrible event that took place September 11, 2001. Standing outside, at one particular event, the sky was clear just like it was that day. Watching the birds fly over and listening to the silence I couldn't help but feel God's presence. I will never know what many went through that day, but I pray God's presence was there. We all want to feel God's presence. Call out to Him and ask Him to comfort you wherever you are.

Psalm 86:7 "In the day of my trouble I will call to you, for you will answer me."

September 12

Wait for Him

At a time in my life when I was looking for a new job, I couldn't help but want something to happen quickly. I had to remind myself many times that it wasn't for my benefit, but for His. God's timing is perfect and if we wait for Him to lead us, our blessings will be even greater.

Psalm 73:28 "But as for me, it is good to be near God. I have made the sovereign Lord my refuge; I will tell of all your deeds."

September 13

Pray for Understanding

It's easy to get frustrated, when an appointment we scheduled months ago, gets cancelled. When things like that happen, we don't always know the reasons behind them. Many times, we only think about how it is affecting us. What if I told you it was cancelled because the doctor just found out he had cancer? Your schedule might be changed suddenly, but remember that it's only a minor thing, compared to some of the reasons behind those changes. Don't get frustrated, instead, pray for understanding and ask God to be with everyone involved.

Romans 8:18 "I consider that our present sufferings are not worth comparing with the glory that will be revealed in us."

September 14

Life Changing

I have heard so many wonderful things from people who have experienced an overseas mission trip. They've talked about how life changing it is. How wonderful it must be...helping those in need, sharing God's great news and being able to grow spiritually, when you realize what's really important.

Psalm 67:2 "that your ways may be known on earth, your salvation among all nations."

Galatians 6:9 "Let us not become weary in doing good, for at the proper time we will reap a harvest if we do not give up."

September 15

I've Got You

I don't remember learning how to walk but I know my parents and family were there saying "I've got you," every step of the way. When I learned how to ride my bike, I remember them saying "I've got you," each time we would try it. Isn't it great that in every moment of our lives, God is there? He's across the room waiting for you to walk to Him. He's behind you, knowing that you might not get there without making mistakes. We might stumble and even fall down at times, but remember God is there every step of the way saying "I've got you."

Psalm 73:23 "Yet I am always with you; you hold me by my right hand."

September 16

Give Him the Recognition

Isn't it nice to be recognized for doing something good? Everyone wants to succeed at something. When you are recognized, do you acknowledge who got you there? Don't forget to thank God and give Him the recognition He deserves. When you're waiting for the success or recognition, ask Him to help you be at peace with what you are doing. In every instance, give it your all knowing He is with you every step of the way.

Psalm 26:12 "Lord, you establish peace for us; all that we have accomplished you have done for us."

September 17

Caring Enough to Pray

When you stop and think about it, praying is actually a pretty easy thing you can do for someone else. If you are worried about someone in your family or someone at work or at school, stop right now and pray for them. Sometimes we want to help but we don't know how we can or what to do. Ask God to speak to them. Ask Him to help you know what to say or what to do for them. Ask Him to help you continue to pray for them. Caring enough to pray for someone, could make all the difference.

Psalm 106:44 "But He took note of their distress when He heard their cry."

September 18 (Part 1)

Let's Talk

As we move into a world full of improved technology and electronics, the way we communicate with each other has changed as well. Many people don't talk face to face anymore, and some don't even talk on the phone. Instead, many of us are communicating by e-mail and text. Isn't it great knowing we can still communicate with God the "old fashioned way?" Talk to Him; let Him know you're thinking of Him right now.

Psalm 118:28 "You are my God, and I will give you thanks; you are my God and I will exalt you."

September 19 (Part 2)

If You Can't Say Anything Nice

Our youth pastor once mentioned the reason people text things they wouldn't normally say out loud, is because the text message doesn't seem real. It is real though, very real! The feelings on the other end are just as emotional as the feelings on your end. Make every effort to only send nice messages and remember, if you can't say anything nice...don't say anything at all...and don't text it either.

Proverbs 4:24 "...keep corrupt talk far from your lips."

September 20

How Wise It Is

As we grow older it's easy to think we don't need our parents anymore. We're old enough to make our own decisions; we don't need to listen to them anymore...right? We often think this as get older, but listening to our parents shows such wisdom, such obedience. How wise it is to show God the utmost respect He deserves, by listening and obeying your parents, as well as all of His commands.

Proverbs 9:12 "If you are wise, your wisdom will reward you..."

September 21

God Wants You Doing and Being Your Best

I have had several very powerful moments in my life when I knew God was with me. I knew He was working through me! There is nothing more powerful than knowing you are right where He wants you, doing right what He wants you to do. Work hard each day knowing God wants you doing your best and being your best. When you don't think you have it in you, let Him know you need His help. He's waiting for you to ask!

Psalm 88:1 "O Lord, the God who saves me, day and night I cry out before you."

September 22

Stick with It

Discipline is a hard thing sometimes. It's hard to receive discipline, especially when we get something taken away that we really enjoy. Harder yet is giving the discipline! Deciding the punishment to fit the "crime" isn't always easy. The main thing to remember though, is to stick with it. Be consistent and fair, loving but firm. Always remind them lovingly how God wants us to live.

Proverbs 4:10 "Listen, my son, accept what I say and the years of your life will be many."

September 23

How Big Is Your Family?

Families are made up of so many different scenarios. Some families are many and some are few, but when love is in the home, they are all families. Whether there are 2 or 8 or 18 in your family, God loves you and wants you to share that love with your family, His family.

Genesis 50:21 "So then, don't be afraid. I will provide for you and your children."

September 24

Try It and Accomplish It

A book I once read talked about going an entire day without criticizing, gossiping or complaining. It doesn't sound that hard, does it, but it's not easy. We have the capability to do it; we just need the right frame of mind. Pray and ask God to help you have a pure heart, so that you can try it and accomplish it.

Psalm 15:2 "...who speaks the truth from his heart and has no slander on his tongue, who does his neighbor no wrong and casts no slur on his fellowman..."

Psalm 15:5 "...He who does these things will never be shaken."

September 25

You Can Change Their Outlook

Have you ever stopped to think about how your attitude can affect someone else's? Pay attention the next time you are in a really good mood. With just a smile you can change someone else's outlook on their day. The opposite can happen as well! When you're having a bad day, it can turn someone else's good day around. Pray God can help you change their outlook, by allowing you to share Him, through your actions and words.

Ecclesiastes 8:15 "So I commend the enjoyment of life, because nothing is better for a man under the sun than to eat and drink and be glad. Then joy will accompany him in his work all the days of the life God has given him under the sun."

September 26

He Knows What You Are Capable Of

Do you sometimes wish that your boss could walk in your shoes for a day? Maybe he or she could do your job and see what it involves. Maybe you feel like you're not appreciated. It's important to remember who you're working for. God knows what you go through every day and He knows what you are capable of. One day we'll all be judged by the same "boss," so do your work every day knowing you're doing it for Him."

Dictionary of NIV terms: Judgement = A decision from God, especially the final judgement when God will reward those who believe in Him.

September 27

Our Lives are Precious

Some members of my family were mourning a loved one's passing when we received word that a new son was born to some of our friends from church. We do not know when our time will be done here on earth. God is the only one who knows that! We can live each day though, remembering how blessed we are to have one another. There are reminders everywhere of how precious our lives are. Therefore, live each day as if it were your last...but also your first.

Ecclesiastes 7:1 "A good name is better than fine perfume, and the day of death better than the day of birth."

September 28

Follow His Lead

I always tell people that I don't know what I want to be when I grow up. The important thing really, is that God knows what He wants me to be. I've had jobs in my life that I know have prepared me for other jobs. I've also had the desire to move on to jobs, that I never would have expected myself doing. Some jobs have come easy and some not so much. No matter where you are in your job or career, content or searching, remember that God has a plan for you. Ask Him to lead you where He wants you. Remember to ask Him to help you be willing to follow His lead.

Job 11:7 "Can you fathom the mysteries of God? Can you probe the limits of the almighty? They are higher than the heavens – what can you do?"

September 29

Live and Learn

I'm sure you've heard the saying "live and learn." God knows we will make decisions that we won't always be happy with. He also knows that we can learn from our mistakes. We should pray that we'll remember those mistakes and not make them again. We need to live our own lives and as we grow older, we can also grow wiser from our lessons learned.

Ecclesiastes 11:9 "Be happy, young man, while you are young, and let your heart give you joy in the days of your youth. Follow the ways of your heart and whatever your eyes see, but know that for all these things God will bring you to judgement."

September 30

You Can Make a Difference

There is no one like you; no other person is exactly like you. You are unique in your own way. You may think you can't make a difference, but you can. Each of us has our own qualities. If we put our minds to something, we can do wonderful things. When we focus our minds on God, there is nothing we can't do.

Romans 12:4-5 "For just as each of us has one body with many members, and these members do not all have the same function, so in Christ we, who are many, form one body, and each member belongs to all the others."

October 1

Is It Really Goodbye?

A TV show I watched once, showed a mom talking about not getting to say goodbye to her son, who had recently died. Have you ever stopped to think about that? Is it really goodbye? It's hard losing a loved one. I don't think you can ever be prepared for it. The good news is, that it doesn't have to be goodbye. God is preparing a place for us, for all of us. He has given us a way to be with our loved ones, for all eternity. Don't let it be goodbye, let God know you want to be with your loved one and Him forever.

Psalm 27:4 "One thing I ask of the Lord, this is what I seek: that I may dwell in the house of the Lord all the days of my life, to gaze upon the beauty of the Lord and to seek Him in His temple."

October 2

I'm Working on It

One day we'll be together in a wonderful place. God is preparing this place, for all of those who love Him and have chosen to live for Him. Can you imagine if He didn't feel like doing it? What if He didn't want to or didn't care. When we go through our day-to-day duties, we should do them with a caring and loving heart. Instead of "why should I" or "I don't want to," we should think about God and what He's doing every day. He's working on it for us, with all the love you could ever imagine. Listen closely; He's saying "I'm working on it…for you."

2 Corinthians 5:1 "Now we know that if the earthly tent we live in is destroyed, we have a building from God, an eternal house in heaven, not built by human hands."

October 3

Lost and Found

I discussed with a good Christian friend of mine once, about how people change. Over the years I think I've changed, at least I hope I have. I hope God has changed me and I pray that He will continue to change me in every way. With God in our lives, we have a purpose to serve and to do His will. I really feel it's the difference between being lost and being found.

2 Corinthians 5:9 "So we make it our goal to please Him, whether we are at home in the body or away from it."

October 4

Have a Good Day

When I was typing an e-mail once, I accidentally typed "Have a God Day." I misspelled good and almost sent it out that way. When I started thinking about it, I felt like that was what I meant anyway, so why not send it that way? I love God and feel so blessed to have Him in my life. I wish everyone could experience that same feeling. I want everyone to know Him and love Him just as I do. I want them and all of you to experience God every day. When you go about your day, this day and every day, remember you don't have to settle for just a good day, when you can have God in your day.

Isaiah 63:9 "...In His love and mercy He redeemed them; He lifted them up and carried them all the days of old."

October 5

What Would You Pray For?

The story of King Solomon really inspires me. Imagine God coming to you in a dream and telling you, that you could have anything you prayed for. He could have prayed for anything, any amount of money or fame. What did he pray for? He prayed for wisdom. With wisdom He could do so much more. I often think about how wise that prayer was. How wise He was to ask for wisdom. Had God already answered his prayer before he even asked?

1 Kings 4:29 "God gave Solomon wisdom and very great insight, and a breadth of understanding as measureless as the sand on the seashore."

October 6

These People Are...

Have you ever heard someone say "these people are so silly" or "what are these people doing?" Have you ever said those phrases or something like it? The next time you want to make a similar comment, remember where we all come from and who we are. Since we are all sinners, we should not be knocking each other down but lifting each other up. Try saying "these people are...God's children," or "these people are...just like me."

Ecclesiastes 7:20-22 "There is not a righteous man on earth who does what is right and never sins. Do not pay attention to every word people say or you may hear your servant cursing you-for you know in your heart that many times you yourself have cursed others."

October 7

Relax and Reflect

I've had days when I wanted to do things for others and other days when I didn't want to much at all. It's okay to take time to relax. Everyone needs time to reflect and time to just do nothing, if that's what you want to do. Sometimes I feel guilty about taking time for myself, but I remember even God rested during His most important work. He rested, then He continued, knowing He would be doing His best work. Have you taken a break lately?

Genesis 2:2 "By the seventh day God had finished the work He had been doing; so on the seventh day He rested from all His work."

October 8

God Made Us in His Image

Someone made a comment to me about my outer appearance once and I struggled with it most of that morning. When I prayed about it, God helped me to remember that we shouldn't look at and determine who someone is by their outer appearance anyway. God made us in His image, capable of being very loving and kind, but most of all, capable of forgiveness. These qualities all come from within. They are with us no matter what we look like. We can pray and ask God for an increased measure of these qualities, when we need them to forgive words we might struggle with.

Psalm 133:1 "How good and pleasant it is when brothers live together in unity."

October 9

Please Hold

Aren't you glad that when you pray, God doesn't put you on hold? You can pray anytime, anywhere and God will be listening. God loves you so much! He will listen intently and lovingly to your every word. Isn't it great to know that you will never get a busy signal, be transferred or be put on hold? Give it a try, call to God, He is always listening.

Psalm 5:1 "Give ear to my words, O Lord."

October 10

Peace Instead of Panic

I have had many times in my life when I had anxiety over something. I've been nervous about speaking in front of a crowd of people. I've been anxious when awaiting important news. My cousin reminded me how nervous you can get before a test. Some people have even mentioned to me, that they aren't good at taking tests. Even when they know the answers, they just get too nervous. It's important to pray in all areas of your life. It's okay to ask God for peace and comfort to get you through those times. When you're relaxed, you can do your best and stay focused on the task, not the anxiety. Ask God to help you have peace so you don't have to panic.

2 Thessalonians 3:16 "Now may the Lord of peace himself give you peace at all times and in every way. The Lord be with all of you."

October 11

An Emotional Rollercoaster

Have you ever had emotions come over you that you couldn't control? Our lives are full of surprises and sometimes we don't know what our day will be like. Maybe your day started off good but your co-worker's day didn't. You walk into work happy to be there –them- not so much. Which one of you will end up letting your emotions take over? Will your good mood be enough to help them change their day around? Don't ride the emotional rollercoaster. Choose to start each day with prayer to control your emotions. Pray you can stay true to who you are and ask God to help you remain Christlike, no matter what your daily rollercoaster ride is like.

1 Thessalonians 4:13 "Live in peace with each other."

1 Thessalonians 4:15 "Make sure that nobody pays back wrong for wrong, but always try to be kind to each other and to everyone else."

October 12 (Part 1)

Each of Us Has Different Qualities

I have a big family, who I am very close to. Growing up, I always felt like I had my best friends living with me. As an adult and even more so, as a Christian I realize how blessed I've been. Not one of us is the same, but we're all loved by the same parents. Do I love any one of them more than the other? No. I do go to them for different things at different times, though. It's wonderful seeing the different qualities each one of us has. Not one of us is the same. God made us all different and I couldn't imagine it any other way.

Romans 12:6 "We have different gifts, according to the grace given us."

October 13 (Part 2)

Each One His

My parents have 7 children. The wonderful thing about my parents, is the love they have shown us, throughout our lives. They have done many things for us and sacrificed even more. We've been through a lot together, but have always come through with love and respect for each other. All of us different, but loved all the same. Imagine what God must be thinking when He sees all of His children. Each one unique, each one special, each one His!

Ephesians 4:7 "But to each one of us grace has been given as Christ apportioned it."

October 14

Like Father

You've probably heard the saying "Like father, like son." Maybe you've said it or someone has said it to you. Have you ever really stopped to think about what it means? Maybe your father has taught you everything he knows about fishing or working on a car or even cooking. What about the qualities you pick up from your parents just from watching them? There are so many things our parents can teach us. Will you listen to your mom… your dad… your Father?

2 Corinthians 6:18 "I will be a Father to you, and you will be my sons and daughters, says the Lord Almighty."

October 15

A Gift from Heaven

A friend of mine decided to have a baby late in life. Babies are such a blessing, whenever you decide to have them. What a great reminder of God's power in His work. God knows how capable of love we are and He shares it with us, in this way. Whether you are carrying a baby, raising a baby, babysitting for someone or looking forward to one day having a baby, remember they are a gift from heaven. They are full of God's grace and love, innocent and special, each one unique in its own way.

John 1:13 "Children born not of natural descent, nor of human decision or a husband's will, but born of God."

October 16

Stop It from Spreading

Rumors and gossip are so powerful! They can ruin someone's day, sometimes even their career. Don't get wrapped up in talking about others or spreading rumors. Put yourself in their shoes, think about how it would hurt you. God made them with the same love and grace He made you with. When you hear gossip about someone, be the first person to stop it from spreading. Isn't that what you would want someone to do for you?

Proverbs 15:4 "The tongue that brings healing is a tree of life, but a deceitful tongue crushes the spirit."

October 17

Who Will Rescue Me?

"I can't go to church, I'm not good enough." We've probably all said this or thought it at some point in our lives. Feeling this way is normal, however nothing is further from the truth. I know you might be hurting right now! We all have times in our lives when we don't feel very Christ like. God's word can help you stay focused on doing what's right. If you haven't been baptized, ask someone to pray with you about it. Better yet, pray to God right now! Ask him to come into your heart.

Lord, I don't feel good enough, I want to be better. I know you can help me in every way. Please give me the confidence I need to go to church. I want to have your word in my heart. I want to be with other people that understand that no one is perfect and that we all need you. I pray this in your son's name, Amen!

Romans 7:24 "What a wretched man I am! Who will rescue me from this body of death?"

October 18 (Part 1)

Hold Off on Changing

Some people are easy to get along with, while others are harder to get along with. You may get along with everyone you work with and then all of a sudden, someone starts working there, that makes your day a little more of a struggle. When this happens, hold off on changing your attitude or changing who you are. Pray and ask God to help you remain kind to them and to help you be open-minded. Ask for guidance, so that you will treat them the way you want to be treated. They might need to hear God's word from you or they might have questions, that you can help answer.

Colossians 4:5-6 "Be wise in the way you act toward outsiders; make the most of every opportunity. Let your conversation be always full of grace, seasoned with salt, so that you may know how to answer everyone."

October 19 (Part 2)

God Places People in Our Lives for a Reason

Have you ever wondered why God puts certain people in your life? Maybe you get along with some and share a lot of time with them. You might share your struggles and pray with each other. What about those you have a harder time getting to know? Do you often wonder if they pray? Remember, God places people in our lives for a reason. Perhaps they need our help with something or our prayers. Perhaps we need theirs! Whatever the reason, try to get to know them, pray for them and learn to love them.

Colossians 3:12 "Therefore, as God's chosen people, holy and dearly loved, clothe yourselves with compassion, kindness, humility, gentleness and patience."

October 20

Pray About it and Forget it

There will be times in your life when you won't know which road to take. Maybe you're thinking of changing careers or wondering whether or not to go to college. We make decisions daily, often wondering if we've made the right choices. Don't stress yourself out over which road to take. Pray about it and forget it! God will answer your prayers. When you ask Him for an answer, ask Him to make it obvious what road you should take.

Colossians 4:2 "Devote yourselves to prayer, being watchful and thankful. "

Colossians 4:4 "Pray that I may proclaim it clearly, as I should."

October 21

Feel His Presence

Someone once asked me if I was excited about some news I had received. On the inside, I was beaming! I was thanking God for His answers to prayer, knowing He had answered them in His perfect timing. On the outside, it probably seemed to others that I was nonchalant about the news. I knew God had everything to do with it, and He was leading me where He wanted me. It was calming to know, that God was in control. Pray and ask God to help you feel confident in all areas, so that you can feel at ease, by feeling His presence.

2 Thessalonians 3:5 "May the Lord direct your hearts into God's love and Christ's perseverance."

October 22

There Are No Coincidences

I watched a show once about angels. Some people couldn't explain where their strength came from during their struggles. Many different stories were shared with many different outcomes. I realized I've had moments in my own life where I know I had help. I think that it's easy to chalk it up to coincidences. God set a plan in place and He will make it happen if it is His will for us. You may not see it when you're going through it. When you reflect back on it, though, I bet you'll see the many miracles that were made along the way, for His good.

Luke 2:13-14 "Suddenly a great company of the heavenly host appeared with the angel, praising God and saying "Glory to God in the highest, and on earth peace to men on whom His favor rests."

October 23

Admit It

Whenever you're in a situation where you've messed up, admit it! When you admit it up front, that you did something wrong, it stops the gossip before it starts. Maybe you were late to work or you didn't help with that big project everyone else worked on. Everyone has an "off" day, a day where things aren't always what you meant them to be. It's not like you and you want to make it better. Admit it up front! You'll enjoy having a clear mind because you turned it around and did the right thing. When people know that it's not like you to do wrong, they'll appreciate you admitting it to them. Admitting you're wrong is not a sign of weakness, it is a sign of strength. When others want to know where your strength comes from, tell them…admit it!

Proverbs 13:10 "Pride only breeds quarrels, but wisdom is found in those who take advice."

October 24

Sacrificing for Others

There are many jobs to choose from. You'll have jobs you expected to do, jobs you hoped you'd get to do and jobs you never dreamed you'd be doing. The world offers us many opportunities and thankfully, we'll all choose different jobs at different times. We all need each other and sometimes we have to sacrifice something. What if Jesus never sacrificed for us? What if He hadn't wanted to take up the cross? Thankfully, Jesus did sacrifice for us. He did not turn away from us because He loves us. Do your job with love in your heart. Love the fact that you are blessed with an opportunity to help someone else do their job. Love the thought of fulfilling God's will. Each job truly does have a purpose.

Ecclesiastes 2:24 "A man can do nothing better than to eat and drink and find satisfaction in His work. This too is from the hand of God."

October 25

You'll Feel Better in The Long Run

Sometimes, it's hard to tell the truth, especially if you think you'll get in trouble. Kids tell lies or don't admit they did something wrong because they think it will keep them from getting into trouble. The truth comes out sooner or later, so it is better to come clean with the truth right away. Your life at any age, will go smoother, when you tell the truth. You'll feel better in the long run, knowing also, that it's the right thing to do.

Proverbs 12:17 "A truthful witness gives honest testimony, but a false witness tells lies."

October 26

You Can Live Life in a New Way

Doesn't the idea of being born again sound comforting? Imagine being able to "do-over" your mistakes and live life in a new way; a way where you can see clearer and know the difference between right and wrong. When you accept Jesus in your life, you have the chance to be born again. Jesus gave you a way to be forgiven for your sins, so you can live life in a new way. God loves you so much! He wants you to be able to live with a clear heart. Ask Him to help you have the confidence to come forward, so that you can live life in a new way.

John 3:5 "Jesus answered, 'I tell you the truth, no one can enter the Kingdom of God unless he is born of water and the spirit."

John 3:7 "You should not be surprised at my saying 'You must be born again.'"

October 27

Do Not Be Afraid

Do your fears stop you from getting out and helping others? Do you wish you could help, but are not sure if you can do it? Maybe you don't think you'll know what to do. God wants you to help others. He wants you telling others about Him. When you aren't sure if you have what it takes, put your trust in Him. Ask God to take over and give you what you need. Ask Him for the courage and the strength to step out of your comfort zone. Pray to God, for what you need and watch Him work wonders in your life, so that you can help others.

Exodus 14:13 "Do not be afraid. Stand firm and you will see the deliverance the Lord will bring you today."

October 28

Wherever You Go

It can be scary looking for a new job. What about a job you've never done before; a job you never expected you'd be doing? God has a plan for us and sometimes that plan seems scary. Maybe we don't think we have what it takes to get the job done. Maybe we think we'll fail. God's plan for you is no mistake. He'll give you what you need to get the job done and He'll never let you fail.

Joshua 1:16 "…Whatever you have commanded us we will do, and wherever you send us we will go."

October 29

He Will Be There

It saddens me sometimes to think that we can't speak of God in public schools. God is there though, as long as we keep Him there. Take Him there with your prayers. Share Him with others by praying for them. Show Him to everyone with your kindness. I am thankful to have had the support of Christian co-workers that I worked with at an Elementary school. I'm so glad they were not afraid to pray for others. It's important to remember that where you are, He is with you, He will be there!

Nehemiah 1:11 "O Lord, let your ear be attentive to the prayer of this your servant and to the prayer of your servants who delight in revering your name. Give your servant success today by granting him favor in the presence of this man."

October 30 (Part 1)

Let Him In

I am always glad to see so many people on Facebook and other social media platforms, who aren't afraid to share their faith. I love seeing prayer requests when people call upon others for prayer and comfort. To me that is what it's all about! It's okay to admit you can't do it on your own. It's okay to let others in.   When you ask people for support in prayer, you are truly inviting Him in to help you. He wants you to give it to Him. Don't be afraid to let others in. Most of all, don't be afraid to let Him in.

1 Thessalonians 1:3 "We continually remember before our God and Father your work produced by faith, your labor prompted by love, and your endurance inspired by hope in our Lord Jesus Christ."

October 31 (Part 2)

Remind Each Other

A friend of mine posted a saying on Facebook from a very popular Christian author. I was impressed by the amount of people that "liked" the comment. I love seeing Christians not afraid to talk freely about where their faith comes from. I believe it's important for us to remind each other, who to turn to and who we need to thank. I am thankful I get the chance to talk freely about my hope and faith. I have always enjoyed reading and writing. Ever since I can remember I have wanted to be a writer. I pray that the words you read in these devotions, will remind you what's important, so that you can remind others. I pray it reminds you "who" is important and that you too are not afraid to share His word.

Daniel 9:18 "...We do not make requests of you because we are righteous, but because of your great mercy."

November 1

What's on Your Heart?

"I've gone to church my whole life and still struggle with this." This was a quote I saw on Facebook in response to a friend's post. "Turning it over to Him" was the subject and as we all know, that is easier said than done. We all struggle with this, but why? Maybe we are too proud and don't want to admit we can't do it on our own. Maybe we aren't sure how to turn it over to God or where to begin. Why not begin each day in prayer, letting Jesus know you are ready to follow Him.

Lord, thank you for all you do for us! As we go about our day, help us to be pleasing to you. We want to do what's right in all situations, most of all, for you. Whatever is on our hearts today, help us to turn it over to you. I pray this in your son's name, Amen!

Exodus 14:14 "The Lord will fight for you; you need only to be still."

November 2

24/7

We've all seen these numbers together in advertisements and reminders. We also use them to speak of work or our busy schedules. When you think about it, though, none of us are truly busy or even available 24 hours a day, 7 days a week. None of us are constantly working or even awake all the time. We rest, we sleep, we read, we write, we might play games or take time off. The point is we are only human and will remain that way until we are called home. However, there is someone who is available for you 24/7. Think about it, day or night, all day, every day, God is here for you. He's waiting for you to talk to Him, waiting and listening and already knowing what you need. Pray to God anytime, pray to Him ALL the time. He truly is available for you 24/7.

Nehemiah 1:6 "let your ear be attentive and your eyes open to hear the prayer your servant is praying before you day and night."

November 3

Turn It Off

It's unfortunate that so many television shows have inappropriate language and subject matters. Watching TV with my children, when they were young, it was a shame having to explain so many matters, that shouldn't have been shown on a "family" show. Many times, I talked with them about situations or words that were brought up. TV has changed a lot over the years. I find myself just turning it off most of the time. It's so much more peaceful to me, not having the TV on. Ask God to help you and your family make wise choices with the shows that are on. When it's not an appropriate subject matter, ask Him to help you turn it, better yet, ask Him to help you turn it off.

Matthew 6:22 "The eye is the lamp of the body. If your eyes are good, your whole body will be full of light."

November 4

Follow Your Heart

I was talking to a fellow Christian about getting to the point in our lives, when we not only believed in Jesus, but truly began a relationship with Him. It was a good discussion and as she put it, nice to realize that we don't just have Jesus in our head, but we have found Him in our hearts. If you are struggling with this, ask Jesus to come into your heart. Let Him know, that you not only believe in Him, but you want to know Him. Ask Him to help you follow your heart.

Ecclesiastes 3:11 "He has made everything beautiful in its time. He has also set eternity in the hearts of men; yet they cannot fathom what God has done from beginning to end."

November 5 (Part 1)

Stick to What's Important

During our lifetime, we'll set many different goals. I remember setting goals when I started writing these devotions. When the goals didn't work out, I didn't stress on it though. I realized the words weren't mine anyway, and I didn't want them to be. I wanted them to be messages to you from God. I wanted the goals to be His. When you are in a situation where you have goals, pray and ask God what He has in mind. Ask God to lead you and to help you stick to what's important...His goals!

Psalm 119:30 "I have chosen the way of truth; I have set my heart on your laws."

November 6 (Part 2)

Let Him Be Your Goal

Several times I have set out to read the bible in a year. Many have done it and many more will accomplish it. As I am writing these words, I have not yet finished the entire reading in a year's time. I have however, found other ways to get involved with reading the bible regularly. Someone on the radio once made a good point about setting a goal like reading the bible in a year. Don't go into it looking to finish, go into it looking for wisdom. Ask God to help you seek Him when you read the bible, not to seek the deadline. Whether you finish it in a year or not, just make sure you're reading it for the right reasons. I always find that I feel better when I'm reading the bible regularly for the purpose of learning more about God. Shouldn't that be our goal?

Proverbs 4:25 "Let your eyes look straight ahead, fix your gaze directly before you."

November 7

What's in Your Eyes?

Sharing Jesus with someone in their time of need can be very moving; especially when God gives you the words and actions and you know He's working through you. A co-worker once told me about a time when they shared Jesus with someone in their time of need. A woman came to her one night asking some tough questions. She knew only God would be able to help her give the right answers. In the end, the woman in need asked her, "Is that what I see in your eyes? Is that Jesus?" How amazing that even in her time of need and during a time of darkness she could see the hope in someone else's eyes.

Luke 10:23 "...Blessed are the eyes that see what you see."

November 8

His Amazing Ways

We've all heard the saying "God moves in mysterious ways." We should say "God moves in amazing ways." It's amazing to me how God moves in our lives. He brings us together with people of different backgrounds, different personalities and different opinions, for His purpose. We do our best work when we are doing our work for Him. Embrace the differences that God places in your path. Know that God is working through you to fulfill His purpose, His amazing mysterious purpose.

Psalm 47:2 "How awesome is the Lord most High, the great King over all the earth."

November 9

I Do Better with Christ

My husband was getting ready to go to the store and asked me what toothpaste I wanted. I immediately said "I do better with Christ." I had meant to say "Crest" but how awesome to have those words come out without even thinking about it. It's true…I do better with Christ in my life. In that moment, I took it as a reminder. I hope and pray that I will continue to be reminded of the fact that things in my life go much better when I put my focus on Him. I pray that you will be reminded of Him each and every day too.

Jeremiah 1:9 "…Now I have put my words in your mouth."

November 10 (Part 1)

The One Who Loves Us

It's easy to look at someone and think they have it easy. Maybe it seems they have a lot of money or don't have any problems. The truth is we never really know what anyone else is going through. We all have different things we go through and different ways we handle them. At the end of the day, and really any time at all, I hope we all turn it over to the one who loves us, no matter what. He knows our thoughts and our troubles. He knows what we need and will give us the strength we need, to get through it all.

Joshua 1:7 "Be strong and courageous…"

November 11 (Part 2)

He Will Get You Through It

Sometimes I think my life is tough or a situation I'm going through is hard and then reality sets in. I'll watch the news or hear about something that I can't even imagine going through. For that person, their situation is very real too. They may be wondering how someone else is able to handle what they are going through. Each of our situations is unique...unique to us. God knows and loves us though. Keep praying to God no matter what you are going through and He will get you through it.

Joshua 1:9 "...Do not be terrified; do not be discouraged, for the Lord your God will be with you wherever you go."

November 12 (Part 1)

It's Never Too Late

There was a time in my life when I wanted to have a relationship with an old friend of mine, that I hadn't seen in a long time. I was missing our long talks and how we always knew just what to say to each other. Have you ever had a relationship like that? Have you ever fallen away from a relationship like that? Maybe your relationship with Jesus has been like that lately. If you miss your long talks and want more out of your relationship with Him, it's never too late to seek it.

John 8:47 "He who belongs to God hears what God says."

November 13 (Part 2)

Get in Touch, Stay in Touch

Whenever you think of getting in touch with an old friend, you should just do it. They've probably been thinking about you too. Odds are they have probably thought of getting in touch with you often. There are so many ways to get in touch these days. Modern technology helps you stay in touch easily. The truth is the same about your relationship with Jesus. There are many ways to stay in touch. We can go to church, read the bible, and get involved in prayer groups. There are many, many more ways to stay in touch, especially through prayer. Once you get in touch with Him, you'll want stay in touch!!

Joshua 1:8 "…meditate on it day and night."

Psalm 25:14 (ESV) "The friendship of the Lord is for those who fear Him and He makes known to them His covenant."

November 14

Things Aren't Always as They Seem

I found out some information that changed a situation and I became aware that it was not as it first seemed. I admit I was quick to judge when I had first heard the story. The truth was they had a very good reason for doing what they did. A reason they didn't share with anyone because they wanted to protect someone else. They made themselves look bad to protect another person. They took the blame, the hurt and the shame for that person's sin. Not too many people would sacrifice their reputation like that. The love that shows, like the love Jesus shows us, is a wonderful thing. I learned a lesson and realize I should not have been so quick to judge! In every situation, through all things, let God be the judge. Remember, things aren't always as they seem.

Romans 2:2 "...God's judgement against those who do such things is based on truth."

November 15

Are You Looking?

God shows His love in so many ways; in the actions of others and in the thoughts we have. God is present everywhere we look. He's in the sun, the snow, and any change of weather. Do you look for Him? He's there! It's up to us to look for Him. Don't just look for Him on Sundays, although that's the best place to start. Look for Him in His word, in the beauty He's given us and in each other. Show Him to others with your actions and tell others about Him. Are you looking? He's there!

1 Samuel 12:16 "Now then, stand still and see this great thing the Lord is about to do before your eyes."

November 16

When You Least Expect It

At times in my life I have worried about many things. I've worried about how I would pay a bill and worried about traveling. I've also worried about my job and of course my family's health and safety. Worrying has gotten the best of me many times. It wasn't until I knew Jesus that I realized I didn't have to do it on my own. Whenever I turn my worries over, I find a greater peace. Usually that peace comes when I least expect it. I pray we remember to turn our worries over to God. Let Him give you the peace you need, when you least expect it.

1 Peter 1:3 "Praise be to the God and Father of our Lord Jesus Christ! In His great mercy He has given us new birth into a living hope through the resurrection of Jesus Christ from the dead."

November 17

Storm Warning

Isn't it nice to get a "heads up" when a storm is on its way? We can prepare for storms when we know they are coming. What about when we don't know they are coming? How do we prepare for them then? You can prepare for any storm in your life, whether it is health related, weather related or anything else. By reading and living God's word you can be prepared to take on the biggest storms. Pray and ask God to help you get through the storms you are facing. Allow Him to be your protector before and during any storm warning.

Proverbs 30:5 "Every word of God is flawless; He is a shield to those who take refuge in Him."

Psalm 91:4 "God will protect you."

November 18

When Was the Last Time You Checked In?

My sister once asked me when I had last checked in with my parents. She was concerned, with good reason, that I wasn't checking in enough. How often are you checking in? Do you check in daily/weekly? Are you only checking in when you need something? Checking in with your family to let them know you're okay and to see how they are doing, should be a very important part of your regular routine. The same is true with your Father in heaven. He knows how you are doing, but He still wants to hear from you. He cares about you and wants to hear from you daily. When was the last time you checked in?

Jeremiah 29:13 "You will seek me and find me when you seek me with all your heart."

November 19

I Wouldn't Change a Thing

A friend once asked me "If you could go back and change something in your life, what age would you be?" Years ago, I would have given an age, but now I have a different answer so I told him "I wouldn't change anything. If I were to change something, I might not be the person I am today." He then asked me "well, what's so perfect about you?" He was joking of course...I think! It's not at all that I think I am perfect; I realize I am far from it. I also realize, though that the road I've gone down has led me to a relationship with Jesus. For that I wouldn't change a thing; every mistake, every sin and every choice I've made. I know I am not perfect but I also know that each bridge I've crossed has led me to this relationship and because of that I wouldn't change a thing!

Genesis 35:3 "...who answered me in the day of my distress and who has been with me wherever I have gone."

November 20

Listen Carefully

There are many ways you can be a good friend. Friends are kind to each other. They love each other through good times and bad times too. Friends should also help each other make wise choices. I recently had something pointed out to me about the way I was handling a situation. I could have taken offense to it and refused to listen but I knew she was my friend. Instead, I turned it around into something positive. I figured, if she was able to tell me in an open and honest way, it was because she cared about me. Sometimes I think God does this too. He might tell us something through someone else or nudge us in our thoughts to do the right thing. The wise choice would be to listen. Listen carefully to what He has to say. What better friend could you have, than the one who loves you as much as He does?

Proverbs 5:1 "My son, pay attention to my wisdom, listen well to my words of insight…"

November 21 (Part 1)

Who Do You Try to Please?

When you are with your friends, who do you try to please? Are you thinking of yourself and whether or not you're getting everything you deserve? Do you think of your friends and the way they are behaving? Do you try to be like them even if it's wrong? Do you follow Jesus, no matter what your friends might think? If you answered "yes" to the last question, good for you! Putting God first and following Him above everything else is the way it should be. If your friends are questioning that, pray for them and pray for the strength to continue to be who God wants you to be. Please Him!

Proverbs 13:21 "Misfortune pursues the sinner, but prosperity is the reward of the righteous."

November 22 (Part 2)

Choose Your Friends Wisely

How do you choose your friends? Do you look for someone who will make you laugh? Do they follow the rules? What about scripture? Is it important to them? Do they follow it in their actions? When you choose your friends, do you stay true to who you are? Do you stay true to God's word? I know it's hard to always do what's right, but choosing friends who make wise choices is the right step. Choose your friends wisely! Stay true to who you are and stay true to who God wants you to be.

Proverbs 3:20 "He who walks with the wise grows wise, but a companion of fools suffers harm."

November 23

Distinguish Between Right and Wrong

Making choices that you can live with, is an everyday battle. When there are other people you have to make choices for, it's not always easy. Maybe you have kids or you're helping make choices on your parent's behalf. Whenever you have choices to make, remember you never have to make them on your own. Pray you'll make the right decisions for all involved. Ask God to help you see a clear answer to your prayers so you can distinguish between right and wrong.

1 Kings 3:9 "So give your servant a discerning heart to govern your people and to distinguish between right and wrong."

November 24

Like Only a Parent Could Do

No matter how old I get there are still times in my life when I'm talked to a certain way and I withdraw. I feel like a child who needs her parents and wants to be comforted with words and actions that only a parent could give. Have you ever been in a situation where someone spoke to you a certain way or said something to you that made you feel helpless? When that happens, go ahead and turn to your parent. Turn to your Father, who loves you unconditionally. He will comfort you in your time of need, like only a parent could do.

Psalm 103:13 "As a father has compassion on his children, so the Lord has compassion on those who fear him..."

November 25

True Peace

I was talking to someone that had been through a lot in her life. Her story made me feel sad, but I kept listening. She talked about how her family grew apart from her. They were blaming her for everything that had happened. Listening to her story made me feel sorry for her at first. But then, as she continued to talk, she spoke more and more about her spiritual journey. She had come to a place in her spiritual walk where she was filled with contentment. I no longer felt sad for her. I felt joy because of the obstacles she had overcome in her life. As a believer, she had found true peace in Him!

Psalm 119:165 "Great peace have they who love your law, and nothing can make them stumble."

November 26

Give Thanks to the Lord

Do you ever stop to think about everything you are thankful for? We live busy lives and it's easy to forget to count our blessings. Each day is brand new; we never know what's going to take place day to day. When you get up each day, start your day off right. It's a new day to be thankful for a fresh start. At the end of your day, be thankful for the many paths you were able to go down and everything God brought you through. Praise God for the chance to do it all again tomorrow.

Psalm 136:1 "Give thanks to the Lord, for He is good. His love endures forever."

November 27 (Part 1)

Protect Our Children

As a mother I know what it feels like to be concerned for my children. I want to teach them everything I know. I want them to be safe and to make good choices. I want them to really listen and learn from their mistakes. While we can't always be with our kids, there is someone who can be. I pray that God will be with my children as they continue to venture out more and more on their own.

Lord, please protect our children from making bad choices. Help them set clear paths for themselves. Come into their hearts so they will want to be more Christlike in all their ways. I pray this in your son's name. Amen!

Psalm 121:7 "The Lord will keep you from all harm – He will watch over your life..."

November 28 (Part 2)

Don't Give Up on Your Child(ren)

A mother once mentioned to me that she didn't know what else to do to help her child. "After all," she said "I take her to church." Going to church is the first step. It's a wonderful step toward helping your children. What else can you do? Do you pray for God to speak to them? Do you pray God will protect them and keep them safe? I love it when people tell me they are going to church and taking their children to church. Don't let it stop there! Read and study God's word and pray for them daily. Know that it may not always be easy, but it will be worth it. Remember, no matter what, don't give up on your child, God hasn't!

Psalm 121:8 "...the Lord will watch over your coming and going both now and forevermore."

November 29

He Is Able

A prayer request I received once said "God is able" at the end of it. That is so true! He is able to answer our prayers. I have seen His work and am so amazed at what He can do. Never give up on Him! Keep asking for that healing and keep asking for that protection, only He can give you. Believe that He is with you and that He can answer your prayers. Most of all, believe He is able.

Daniel 2:23 "I thank and praise you, O God of my fathers; You have given me wisdom and power, you have made known to me what we asked of you…"

November 30

God Can Help You Help Them

God brought me to a ministry where I saw and heard many sad stories. I also prayed for and with many women and children and their families. Many tears were shed and many lives were changed. The greatest thing about God being involved in this ministry was seeing these families change. Seeing them change from looking so lost to seeing hope fill their eyes. When their tears changed from tears of sadness to tears of joy, only He can be responsible for that. Ask God to help you change. Pray that you can help others change as well.

Job 4:3 "Think how you have instructed many, how you have strengthened feeble hands."

December 1

In More Ways Than One

Isn't it wonderful that there are truly so many ways to help someone find their way to God? Of course, praying for them is at the top of the list. You can also show them with your actions. By setting a good example and making wise decisions, you can help others get to a brighter point in their lives. You can live a more carefree life too. When you live and have a relationship with Jesus and grow close to God, peace finds you. When you reflect that peace for others to see they'll want to learn more about it. They'll want to know more about you and more about Him. You can live a life of peace and you can help reflect that peace to others, in more ways than one.

Job 4:4 "Your words have supported those who stumbled; you have strengthened faltering knees."

December 2

Do It Yourself

There are a lot of "Do It Yourself" guides on just about any subject you can think of. Whenever I do projects on my own, I like to research the task at hand before I get started. My kids used to help me search "Do It Yourself" information on the internet when they were younger. Isn't it great to know that you don't really have to do anything by yourself? You can read about your projects in various books and on the internet. You can even ask others who have done similar projects. Now, imagine a book about everything you need to know. A book that will help you do everything you need to do and has all the information you'll ever need. If you decide to "Do It Yourself," make sure you're reading the bible, so you know everything you need to know and have everything you need. Isn't it great to know, that with God's word, you'll never have to do anything by yourself?

Psalm 119:34 "Give me understanding, and I will keep your law and obey it with all my heart."

December 3

Awards and Rewards

There are many types of awards, some are big and some are small. Some are only open to celebrities; others are open to anyone at any time. Many of us will receive some type of an award in our lifetime, maybe a ribbon during track and field or a certificate for perfect attendance. When you run the race don't think of the material award you might or might not get. Think of the way you'll feel knowing you did your best. Did you show others the way, making the right turns? No matter where you finish, make sure to finish strong. You may not always get the trophy, but with God by your side, you'll get the reward.

James 1:12 "Blessed is the man who perseveres under trial, because when he has stood the test, he will receive the crown of life that God has promised to those who love Him."

December 4

Take My Hand

We all started off in life with someone reaching for us saying, "Take my hand." As infants learning to walk, a hand was extended to us. As we grew and went to school, those hands were there for us when we returned home, waving to us and then hugging us. We've had hands extended to us in many situations and at many different times in our lives. As you recall those memories, imagine the hands that were extended for you when Jesus' arms were outstretched on the cross. God was with you every time you needed a hand and He is with you now. He wants you to accept Jesus in your heart. Jesus was thinking of you as He extended His hands. He's calling for you, saying "Take my hand!"

Psalm 48:10 "Like your name, O God, your praise reaches to the ends of the earth; your right hand is filled with righteousness."

December 5

Where Your Courage Comes From

Many stories in the bible teach us about courage. I often think of how Daniel did not stop praying to God just because of a law. He faced a fear so great because of His belief in God; His belief that everything would be okay if He continued to put His trust in Him. You may not be facing a bunch of lions, but you're probably afraid of something and those feelings are real and can be very scary. Read and study the bible to help you remember where your courage comes from. Ask God to help you face your fear, so you can stand up against any lion.

Daniel 6:23 "...no wound was found on him, because he had trusted in his God."

December 6

The Ultimate Superhero

The DJ was talking on the radio once about how her son was trying to decide what superhero to dress as. He'd selected one and then changed his mind several times over a period of time. Finally, he chose one that he'd made up. When his mom asked him what super power his superhero had the boy said, "All of them." When we're kids our imaginations are endless. We can pretend to have a superhero with every super power possible. Isn't it comforting to know that as we grow and learn about God, we can actually have a superhero that truly does have these amazing powers and more? Who else can see the future and heal and protect us? Who else is able to change our hearts and make us superheroes in someone else's eyes? Don't forget God's powers are endless. Imagine what you can do and who you can be, with Him by your side.

Jeremiah 10:6 "No one is like you, O Lord; you are great, and your name is mighty in power."

December 7 (Part 1)

New and Improved

In this busy world we see a lot of things change. "Improved Technology" and "New and Improved" are just a couple of sayings we see and hear. I'm a big fan of change when it's for the better and it's something that's made to last. Personally, I haven't had much luck with technology over the years. I often wonder why more time isn't spent improving the existing item, rather than making new, smaller electronics that don't seem to last. God made you with the ability to change for the better. Not a new model, just an improved you. God made you with certain qualities that can and will be improved when you trust in Him. Are you following God's will, so you can be the "new and improved" you that He wants you to be?

2 Corinthians 5:17 "Therefore, if anyone is in Christ, he is a new creation; the old has gone, the new has come!"

December 8 (Part 2)

One Thing Will Never Change

As I think about the many things that have changed over the years, I'm glad about one very important thing. I'm glad that there is one thing that has never and will never change. God has always been the same and His love for us will never change. He continues to change us and will continue to bring us closer to Him. He will never leave us and His promises will remain true for all of us. As my life continues to change, I continue to want to change for the better with His help. As I change, I am more and more thankful that God never will.

Revelation 1:8 "'I am the Alpha and the Omega,' says the Lord God, 'who is, and who was, and who is to come, the Almighty.'"

December 9

Keep It Clean!

Have you ever been involved in a conversation you didn't want to be a part of? What about when you've heard something that you wished you hadn't heard? There are times too, when we'll be listening to the TV or radio and there is an inappropriate subject. Even previews push the limits these days with what they talk about on TV. Where do you draw the line? Do you have open conversations with others to let them know that you're uncomfortable with the language they use around you or your children? Do you have regular conversations with your children to help them distinguish between right and wrong in these instances? Our children are very vulnerable and we can be too. Use God's word during this time to help your family stay on track and to help keep the conversations around you clean.

1 Timothy 6:20 "...Turn away from godless chatter and the opposing ideas of what is falsely called knowledge."

December 10

Sooner Rather Than Later

There are times I have prayed about situations and have felt like I had an immediate relief from the anxiety I was feeling. Right away I wondered why I hadn't prayed sooner. I pray regularly, and in many situations, but I'll also be the first to admit that many times I don't put it first. I let my anxieties and worries get the best of me before I'm reminded to pray. Put God first in everything you do. In good times be thankful and In tough times, seek His guidance.   Remember to pray in all situations, sooner rather than later.

Colossians 4:2 "Devote yourselves to prayer, being watchful and thankful."

December 11

Travel Safely

When you travel, what is your goal for getting there? Do you rush through traffic, trying to get there quickly? Do you take it slow, noticing the sights around you? The speed limits that are set, help us get to our destinations quicker than ever before. Think about why you're going through this life in the first place. God has a plan; He wants you arriving at the destination He has planned for you. In a world where most deaths are due to traffic accidents, what are your goals for your travels? Instead of trying to get where you're going so quickly, enjoy the road God has planned for you. Take the twists and turns with Him and work toward arriving in a safe, positive manner. Remember, with God by your side you can travel safely.

Numbers 20:17 "...We will travel along the King's highway and not turn to the right or to the left until we have passed through your territory."

December 12

Respond with God's Words

Technology helps us get information out much quicker than in years past. In some ways this is a good thing. You can get invitations sent out quicker and you can keep in touch with people all over the world. One thing to remember though, is that sometimes it's too quick. Once it's sent it cannot be taken back! It remains there for that person to read over and over again, word for word. Think before you push the "send" button on an e-mail or text. Keep God's word at the focus of all your day to day happenings. Live out God's word and spread His word. When you get an e-mail, don't act on it right away. Rather than responding with your words too quickly, take your time and respond with His word.

Psalm 119:16 "I delight in your decrees; I will not neglect your word."

December 13

Practice Makes Perfect

Trying new things is fun, but sometimes it can be scary. Not knowing the rules to a new game or how you'll do isn't always a good feeling. When you try new things, do you feel comfortable learning the directions or helping others learn? What about meeting new people...are you the type of person that likes to share things about yourself right away or does it take you a while to get to know someone? How about your relationship with God? Do you share all your thoughts with Him? Are you sharing His news with others? God wants you to share what you know about Him. If you don't know where to begin, start by praying about it. The more you do something, the easier it will become. Practice sharing God's word! You'll soon find that this practice makes perfect sense.

Acts 18:9 "Do not be afraid; keep on speaking, do not be silent."

December 14

Life Is Short

Whenever I am down, I like to remember the big picture. Why am I here? What does God have planned for me? Better yet, how does my plan work into someone else's plan? God has done wonderful things in my life and can do the same for you. Some days I want to tell everyone I know about His great work. Other days I want to tell everyone, whether I know them or not. He has a plan for you! Don't wait to find out what the grand plan is. Whether I know you or not, I care what happens to you. If you don't have a relationship with Jesus, let Him know you are ready. Life is too short!

Job 7:7 "Remember, O God, that my life is but a breath..."

December 15

God Only Knows

Have you ever been totally surprised by some news that you received? How do you handle those surprises? Do you accept them with open arms or do you try to resist? Life is full of surprises, some good and some not so good. Whenever you are surprised by news, that you weren't quite expecting, remember to remain focused on God. Ask Him to help you accept the changes that happen throughout your day. God only knows how it's all going to turn out. Turn to Him for guidance and the peace to accept the surprises along the way.

Judges 18:6 "...Go in peace. Your journey has the Lord's approval."

December 16

Learn from Your Mistakes

Have you ever had the urge to do something you knew you shouldn't do? Maybe you have spread news that you shouldn't have. Maybe you said or thought something you wished you hadn't. As we go through life, we're going to make mistakes. Learning from those mistakes is what helps us grow. Ask God to help you do the right thing. Ask Him to help you say the right things. Since our thoughts, sometimes lead to our actions, pray that God will help you have clear and pure thoughts. Most of all, if and when you make mistakes, pray you will learn from them.

Proverbs 24:6 "for though man falls seven times, he rises again..."

December 17

God Is with You

We lost a loved one who had suffered a long time. You can never fully prepare for something like that and it is not an easy thing to go through, no matter when it happens. Shortly after he had passed away, I received a note from a friend, who told me she felt as though she had lost him too. We had shared so many prayers for him over the years. When we pray together and for each other, God is with us. I pray you will find comfort knowing, that your loved ones are with God. In return, remember God is always with you.

Romans 10:13 "for, everyone who calls on the name of the Lord will be saved."

December 18

Respect One Another

I remember once when I was younger; my best friend tripped and fell in my driveway. My immediate reaction was to laugh...which I did! Well, that wasn't the best choice and she let me know that I had hurt her feelings...with good reason. I felt bad; I knew I should have asked if she was okay. I knew that I shouldn't have laughed. We were friends and I let her down. Even if we had been enemies, when I had seen her fall, it wouldn't have been right to laugh. We all have feelings and no matter what our relationship is with the other person, God made us and He wants us to love one another. We should at least love Him enough, to respect one another.

Proverbs 24:17-18 "Do not gloat when your enemy falls; when he stumbles, do not let your heart rejoice, or the Lord will see and disapprove and turn his wrath away from him."

December 19

Thank Him for Taking Care of It

How often do you question why something turned out the way it did? Do you talk to others and question someone's authority, their decision, or their attitude? Many times, I have been guilty of this. A co-worker and I once questioned a decision that changed a placement for someone we cared and worried about. After everything was done, it was nice to look back and see that the decision was for the best. How many times have you looked back and been glad God was in charge? How many times have you looked back and thanked Him for taking care of it?

Romans 9:16-17 "It does not, therefore, depend on man's desire or effort, but on God's mercy. I raised you up for this very purpose, that I might display my power in you and that my name might be proclaimed in all the earth."

December 20

The Perfect Gift

As the year comes to an end, I cannot help but think about all the things I have come through. There have been many ups and downs and I'm glad I haven't had to go through them alone. If you're not in a relationship with Jesus, now is a good time to seek it. Ending the year or starting the New Year with a new perspective would be a wonderful gift. Not only will it make a difference in your own life, you could be giving someone else the idea for this perfect gift.

John 15:5 "I am the vine; you are the branches. If a man remains in me and I in him, he will bear much fruit; apart from me you can do nothing."

December 21

God Did

I heard a story about a child who was asked "what do you need to make you grow?" The question was asked during an assessment, in order to prepare the child for the start of school. Some of the possible answers listed were seeds, the sun, water, soil, etc. However, this child answered "God." I was glad that the evaluators of this test did not have to only accept the possible answers. As long as the answer was within reason and made sense, they could accept it. What a blessing that, not only did this child know God, but thankfully, the evaluator did too.

Genesis 1:9 "And God said, 'Let the land produce vegetation; seed-bearing plants and trees on the land that bear fruit with seed in it, according to their various kinds.'"

December 22

God's Work

I was telling someone about my job at a domestic violence shelter. I get a lot of different reactions when I tell people I worked there. Honestly, after my first interview, I left there and cried. I remember telling God that if He thought I able, then for Him, I was willing. I prayed a lot in those early days and I know and realize it was all through Him and His will that I was brought there. Working there I saw many things, both good and bad. The wonderful thing about it though, was being able to see God's work in it all. God's hand has truly touched so many lives there. It's good to be reminded of His power through the lives that have been changed.

Malachi 4:2 "But for you who revere my name, the sun of righteousness will rise with healing in its wings."

December 23

Accept It

If God came to you today and asked you to follow Him, would you do it? Are you doing it now? God wants you to follow Him each and every day, in every way. Don't just follow Him on Sundays, in Sunday school or at church. Follow Him to work, to school, to your friend's house, when you travel and when you stay home. Don't just put up a front for others, wanting them to think you are a Christian, be a Christian! God knows you're not perfect, but He does want you to come to Him. He accepts you for who you are, accept His invitation today.

Acts 4:12 "Salvation is found in no one else, for there is no other name under heaven given to men by which we must be saved."

December 24

Make One for the Right Reason

Many of us have made New Year's Resolutions. I've made many, with good intentions, but haven't always kept them. We all have it in us to do better and be better. God wants to help us with this. He wants us to keep the resolutions we've made and wants us to succeed. Maybe you want to read the bible in a year, or start doing more for others. No matter what you do, doing it for the right reason is the first step toward making it happen. Think about why you want this change; focus on the outcome, while remaining focused on Him.

Proverbs 20:11 "Even a child is known by his actions, by whether his conduct is pure and right."

December 25

Enjoy His Birthday

I've celebrated many birthdays, but none could ever compare to the celebration that occurs, the day our Savior, Jesus Christ, was born. When you celebrate today, don't forget to reflect on the gift that was given to us on His birthday. We were sent a Savior who loves us so much that He would do anything for us. Through the years, many things have tried to take the place of this celebration. In our hearts we know why we're celebrating. Tell the world you celebrate Jesus' birth. Rejoice for yourself and for those who know Him. Pray that everyone will come to know Him. Enjoy His birthday and celebrate the many new births that have occurred because of it.

Hebrews 1:3 "...After He had provided purification for sins, He sat down at the right hand of the Majesty in heaven."

December 26 (Part 1)

The Best Listener

Have you ever had something you wanted to change about yourself? What if there was a way to change how you acted or the way you felt about certain things? Knowing God is a great place to start. Seek God's wisdom for answers to the questions you're looking for. Do you want to become more patient or be a better listener? It's in you to do these things. The ability is within reach. Ask God to lead you to the answers you need. Do you want to be a better listener; then start with the best listener of them all.

Proverbs 2:1, 5 "My son, if you accept my words and store up my commands within you...then you will understand the fear of the Lord and find the knowledge of God."

December 27 (Part 2)

Read It, Study It, Live It

At a time when I was busy with work and school, I remember I felt very frustrated about things. Have you ever asked yourself how you would ever be able to get everything done? In all my busyness I realized I was leaving out something very important...my time in His word. The answers to my questions are always in His word. It's true that no matter how busy I get, if I make time for Him, my life seems to go smoother. God's word holds the answers to all life's questions. Read it, study it, live it!

Proverbs 2:10 "For wisdom will enter your heart, and knowledge will be pleasant to your soul."

December 28

You're Never at the End of His Word

As the end of this year draws near, I pray that it's not the end of your thoughts and time with God. I pray God will continue to speak to you through His word. Whether you are finishing a devotional or His book, remember you are never truly at the end of His word.

Proverbs 4:5 "Get wisdom, get understanding; do not forget my words or swerve from them."

Romans 10:17 "Consequently, faith comes from hearing the message, and the message is heard through the word about Christ."

December 29

He Wants to Speak to Us

I started writing these devotions to share God's word with my family, specifically my children. As I got more and more involved with writing them, I began to want to share His word with everyone. God wants to speak to all of us and He wants us to share His word with others. I pray you will find a way to share God's word, as well as continue to hear it every day.

Ecclesiastes 12:13 "Now all has been heard; here is the conclusion of the matter: Fear God and keep His commandments, for this is the whole duty of man."

December 30

Reflect His Goodness

When we go through tough times, sometimes it's hard to find the good in things. It's important to remember at all times, though, that as a Christian, others will be looking to you. They will watch how you handle the situation. Pray to God; ask for His help handling any situation, in a Christlike manner. Ask Him for the grace and patience only He can give you, so that you can reflect His goodness for others to see.

Psalm 119:33 "Teach me, O Lord, to follow your decrees; then I will keep them to the end."

December 31

Be Open to All His Possibilities

As each year ends, I always like to think about the New Year and all the possibilities that lie ahead. You can look at each day in the same way, really each and every moment. Just because you had a bad situation arise doesn't mean it has to ruin your whole day, your whole year. Pray God will help you see the good in all things. Ask Him to help you be open to all the possibilities He has to offer. I pray you'll have the courage to follow Him. I pray you'll enjoy every minute of where you are and what you are doing, knowing you have God on your side.

1 Corinthians 2:5 "So that your faith might not rest on men's wisdom, but on God's power."

ACKNOWLEDGMENTS

Scripture verses are from the Holy Bible - New International Version (NIV) unless otherwise noted.

Thank you, God, for allowing me to put these thoughts together. I pray they will be an inspiration to everyone who reads them. Thank you for the inspirational journey you allowed me to go through and for the times you spoke to me while writing this book. I am especially thankful for the April 1st devotion. During a rough time in my life you helped me get back on track and helped me to remember what is important.

Thank you to my family, Tony, Jimmy and Anna Ray, for allowing me to read these out loud to you over the years and for always believing in me. Your support and encouragement helped me to finish what I started. I am so thankful to each of you and love you very much!!

Thank you to my parents and my brother and sisters. I've learned so much from each of you and I am thankful for the friendship and love each of you have shown me through the trials and joys of growing up together.

Thank you to Kelly Satchwill for sharing many books, conversations and prayers with me over the years. You have been such an inspiration in my spiritual journey and my life. You've probably prayed more for this book than I have. I am so thankful for you, in more ways than I can express!

Thank you to everyone at Sheltering Wings for all you do. God Bless everyone who has been through their doors, for one reason or another.

Continued to next page

Thank you to my church family and the many Pastors, staff and volunteers, who have taught me so much at Cornerstone Christian Church. I'm thankful for the words of wisdom, hope, honesty and laughter we've shared over the years.

Thank you to Linda Wells for sharing your stories, so that "What's in Your Eyes" could come to life.

Thank you to Scott Curtis, for sharing the JOY acronym. It's a helpful reminder for putting others first.

Thank you to Merle Teskey, for his comment about the 2 by 4 prayer. May we always remember to ask so openly, for an answer from God.

Thank you to Sandi Hartlieb and many other prayer warriors at Cardinal Elementary School, who helped me pray for this book in its early stages.

Thank you to Betsy Owens! You were such an encouragement to me when I wrote these devotions. You reminded me many times where my strength comes from.

Thank you to Sandi Ballard for your lifelong friendship and your knowledge with publishing. Dreams really do come true!!

Thank you to Jane Snyder for encouraging me and helping me proof and edit many of these devotions. I appreciate your eye for detail and am very thankful for you.

ABOUT THE AUTHOR

Susan Ray found her passion for writing at a very young age.

Born the sixth of seven children, she would often write poetry to express her feelings. Her parents and family have always enjoyed listening to her readings, and still continue to encourage her to this day.

Susan has been married to her husband, Tony for 26 years. He has been right alongside her on this journey as she has been called to share God's news. They have two grown children, Jimmy and Anna, whom they love spending time with and who have been the inspiration behind many of Susan's writing projects. When Jimmy and Anna were younger, Susan also wrote several children's stories, that she enjoyed sharing with them over the years.

When Susan became a Christian, she found a new passion for writing and began writing daily devotionals. The main idea behind those, at first, was to share God's word with her children. The more she wrote and learned about God, she felt called to share the devotions with everyone. Her main purpose in sharing them, is that it is important for everyone to know that the simple truth of God's beautiful gift is offered to everyone.

John 3:16 "For God so loved the world that He gave His one and only Son, that whoever believes in Him shall not perish but have eternal life."

Made in the USA
Lexington, KY
17 October 2019